The Serpent's Tail

A memoir by
Deborah Daulton Thibodeau

2022-SECOND EDITION
WITH PHOTOS

THE SERPENT'S TAIL
A memoir
By Deborah Daulton Thibodeau

Copyright © by Deborah Daulton Thibodeau
Published by: Writers Publishing House
info@writerspubilshinghouse.com

All rights reserved. No part of this book may be reproduced in any manner whatsoever without written permission from the author except in the case of brief quotations embodied in critical articles and reviews

For any information, please address
Deborah Daulton Thibodeau - debthibo@gmail.com

or write to:
Deborah Daulton Thibodeau
PO BOX 1650
Dewey, AZ 86327

ISBN: 978-1-64873-404-5
Printed in the United States of America

REVIEWS

The Serpent's Tail" is a beautifully narrated memoir-in-verse that manages to be both heartbreaking and heartwarming at the same time. Told with unflinching honesty, childlike innocence, and with a deep desire to heal unconscionable wounds, Thibodeau's story glows with resilience and determination. She takes us places-emotional and physical-few will ever experience, or even fathom. Tragedy, abuse, betrayed trust, broken families, brainwashed communities, lost innocence...all are offset by Thibodeau's youthful courage and undeterred faith. Ultimately, The Serpent's Tail is a testament to the human spirit, a tale of hope against all odds.

—John Sibley Williams, author of *As One Fire Consumes Another and Skin Memory*

In the many decades that I have been researching the psychology of evil, the most inhumane cruelty is that of cult masters who order parents to abuse their own children, as "God's will." We can now more fully understand how these evil men operate from an insider's personal perspective. The Serpent's Tail is Deborah Daulton Thibodeau's masterfully composed expose of how she survived physical and psychologic abuse growing up in such a misguided cult community. The good news is this inspiring tale of Deb's childhood victory, of her mental grit, to endure in her young life, this nightmare of religious fervor and distorted theology. She emerged battered but emboldened, books burned but now a book created.

—Philip Zimbardo, Ph.D. Professor Emeritus, Psychology Stanford University author of *The Lucifer Effect*

An absolutely brilliant way to describe a most horrific situation. Each and every phrase paints a thousand pictures, giving the reader a personal glimpse into the thoughts and emotions of the author. The result is a guided tour, a once-in-a-lifetime journey to experience the dark hidden secrets of a destructive cult from early childhood development through coming of age and escape.

—John Andrew Collins Founder, William Branham Historical Research, author of *Preacher Behind the White Hoods*

The Daulton family prior to the move to Arizona – Somerset, Kentucky October 1961

The Serpent's Tail is dedicated in loving memory to those gone too soon but never forgotten. My twin sister, Esther Daulton Dorrington, losing her changed the balance completely, and my nephew, Edward Scott, neither could outrun their nightmares, or find solace in life. To Lillia Loker, another child of The Park, who departed this life too soon. Of course, to my unforgettable, wonderful lionheart, Brother Herb and his wife Sister Grace Lott. They gave me something outside of fear and obedience, helped me bear my ex-communication from other children of The Park, and taught me something of events greater than myself. To daddy and mama who tried to give us a direct path to God, but always knew I would choose a different way. To Susan Daulton, my sister-in-law, silently strong and courageous. She treated my children like her own. To my older sister Doris Scott, wolf pack loyal to her family. To Florence Richardson, the seasoned old ER Nurse, who gave me, an untrained, uneducated teen, my first job in the real world and encouraged me to break free from expectations and keep up the fight to go to college and earn my nursing degree. To Dr. John Caskey, who recognized a naïve teen, eager to learn and took it upon himself to break out autoclaved trays and medical equipment and teach me the meaning of sterile technique after I contaminated his suture tray once too often. He never broke a sterile field that I can remember, even when *one of the nurses, on a dare, untied his scrubs and pulled them down around his knees as he was repairing a laceration in the wee hours of the morning. He was the first person to say to me, "You have a book in you. Someday it will find its way out."*

CONTENTS

CONTENTS	6
Prologue	10
CHAPTER 1 – Suffer the Children	14
CHAPTER 2 - Twinning	16
CHAPTER 3 – Southern Origins	30
CHAPTER 4 – The Weight of a Name	43
CHAPTER 5 - The Great Conversion	48
CHAPTER 6 – Building our Future	57
CHAPTER 7 – Choosing the Path	67
CHAPTER 8 – The Great Arizona Vision	74
CHAPTER 9 – Settling in	80
CHAPTER 10 – Mama, Hearth and Home	93
CHAPTER 11– The Value of Just Enough	104
CHAPTER 12 – The Prophet Visits The Park	117
CHAPTER 13 - Death of The Prophet	133
CHAPTER 14 – Cult Life is Established	136
CHAPTER 15 – Tonsillectomies	141
CHAPTER 16 – Bonding of the Five	154
CHAPTER 17 – A Prickle of Awareness	170
CHAPTER 18 – Prank Gone Wrong	183
CHAPTER 19 – Brutal Lessons	187
CHAPTER 20 – Barbie Doll	209
CHAPTER 21 – Predicament of Birth	212
CHAPTER 22 – Widows of The Park	219
CHAPTER 23 - Book Burning	226
CHAPTER 24 – Blinders	239
CHAPTER 25 – Biggest Snow Fall in Prescott History	241
CHAPTER 26 – Lost Innocence	246
CHAPTER 27 – Assigned Chores	264

CHAPTER 28 – The Devil's Familiar	267
CHAPTER 29 – Projection and Opprobrium	270
CHAPTER 30 – Monopoly and Rebellion	278
CHAPTER 31 – Mama is Thrown Out	285
CHAPTER 32 – The Big Patio	287
CHAPTER 33 – Root Cellars	297
CHAPTER 34 – Sister Joan's Exorcism	301
CHAPTER 35 – Elk's Theater	306
CHAPTER 36 – Runaway	308
CHAPTER 37 – Freedom Train	314
CHAPTER 38 – Rabbit Stew	317
CHAPTER 39 – Efficient Beatings	320
CHAPTER 40 – The Worst Beating	322
CHAPTER 41 – Serpent's Seed	336
CHAPTER 42 – Thread of Insanity	341
CHAPTER 43 – Second Shearing	360
CHAPTER 44 – Brother Herb and Sister Grace	364
CHAPTER 45 – Invictus	395
CHAPTER 46 - Panda	399
CHAPTER 47 – Embracing a New Life	403
CHAPTER 48 – The Classics	417
CHAPTER 49 – No Resistance	421
CHAPTER 50 – Christmas Magic	424
CHAPTER 51 – Russian Dinner Party	432
CHAPTER 52 – Spring in Prescott	436
CHAPTER 53 – Awakened Serpent	441
CHAPTER 54 – Sanctified Poachers	452
CHAPTER 55 – A New Family Arrives in The Park	459
CHAPTER 56 – Brother Herb saves Panda	462
CHAPTER 57 – The Serpent Strikes	467
CHAPTER 58 – No Longer a Child	471

CHAPTER 59 – Jezebel Masquerade	**483**
CHAPTER 60 - Bad Timing	**491**
CHAPTER 61 – Prayer for the Serpent	**501**
CHAPTER 62 – New Year's Eve Wedding	**503**
CHAPTER 63 – Stolen Books	**506**
CHAPTER 64 – Bible Trivia	**516**
CHAPTER 65 – Nathan and Dipsey Doodle	**520**
CHAPTER 66 – Mr. Neely	**524**
CHAPTER 67 – Whiskey Sour	**527**
CHAPTER 68 – Strange Covenants	**529**
CHAPTER 69 – Division and Chaos	**535**
CHAPTER 70 - Going Home Again	**537**
CHAPTER 71 – Leaving Pine Lawn Trailer Ranch	**542**
EPILOGUE	**545**
ACKNOWLEDGEMENTS	**556**
ABOUT THE AUTHOR	**575**
REVIEWS	**3**

The Alicante is a mythical Southwestern serpent thought to feed on breast milk. It is said that this surreptitious reptile, seeks a human source. In order to steal her milk, the serpent places a glamour on the nursing mother while he pacifies the infant with his tail.

Manipulated, enthralled, and devout, our parents took this milk thieving reptile to their breast, and their displaced children were left to suckle the serpent's tail.

Prologue

A good life is about forgiveness and enlightenment. I embraced these principles to pursue the life I chose, but it has taken my lifetime to dismantle the wall of defense mechanisms and mental barriers I created in response to abuse no child should experience. I still live with adjustment disorders now recognized as PTSD.

Childhood memories flicker in my brain like freeze frames. Sometimes when I sleep, they emerge, and I relive the terror and desolation I felt when I realized no one would protect me from a sadistic madman, Brother Leo Mercier, The Servant of The Lord. Sweaty nightmare disassociation makes me worry that the things he said, the names he called me, the deviance he accused me of, might be real. These things had a permanent effect on me, much more so than the injury of physical abuse. Daily, I continue my struggle to prove him wrong, to prove myself worthy. These stanzas became my *"Exposure Therapy"* as I journeyed through the past to bring health and recovery to my future.

I am not motivated by hostility, rather a bond to the children who suffered with me and a deep calling to help people understand, immature emotional experiences are indelible as the blackest ink. Children are singular entities, with intelligence and ability to choose what resonates with them. They are gifted to us to love and guide, but we do not have an automatic right as parents, to indoctrinate them and rob them of their tomorrows.

Reverend William Marrion Branham, an evangelical faith healer, recognized for his catastrophic views concerning the end of the world, and the ultimate destiny of humankind, preached about the second coming, the resurrection of the dead, and final judgment. His revival was quasi-Pentecostal, but his theology was old-world fundamentalism infused with borrowed revelations and his notions of proper Christian conduct, especially for women. Between 1945 and 1965, he held huge religious meetings and became famous worldwide. His tales of childhood stirrings, angelic visitations, and divine revelations, drew people who hoped to experience miraculous healing in his prayer lines. According to his sermons, he was the Prophet of the Hour, imbued with the spirit of Elijah, sent to herald the second coming of Christ. *"The only thing this gift is, is just submitting myself to Him. I don't say nothing. He does the saying. The Prophet always has THUS SAYETH THE LORD, it is always right. Don't question the doctrine! With all your heart, you going to believe it? Then you just believe me!"* He was one of many evangelical faith healers who rose to notoriety but his ministry evolved from the roots of white supremacy. He was ordained by and served in the capacity of assistant pastor to Roy Elonza Davis, a Klansman sprung from Stone Mountain in 1915. Branham assumed his congregants after Davis was imprisoned for his many *unrighteous* endeavors.

This is not Christianity, it is twisted religion, the kind that involves the long con, manipulation and mind control of hopeful, salt of the earth people, looking for something of the supernatural to enhance their life after two world wars, post war poverty, opportunistic illnesses of body and mind, and the advent of The Great Depression. Branham's teachings took on a life of their own and became a religion *"The Message"* which more than 2 million people follow today. His books and recorded sermons are still sent around the world, uncensored of plagiarized doctrine, misogyny, racial discrimination, and apocalyptic destruction.

Brother Leo Mercier and his partner, Brother Gene Goad, acolytes, *"Tape Boys,"* traveled with Brother Branham's ministry to record and distribute taped sermons across the country. *"The Park"* came to fruition when Brother Branham blessed Brother Leo Mercier to take a group of followers to Arizona. He likened it to *"a little Goshen,"* where a chosen few live apart from the world to await the second coming of the Messiah. Thus, we became a communal cult within the larger doctrinal cult. In spite of their good intentions and heartfelt ideals, the people of The Park gradually changed, simple faith in God and the Prophet became something darker, and ultimately our life there became the antithesis of their original plan. If Brother Leo Mercier was not born evil, power corrupted him, and he became evil. He exploited parental vulnerability, and they gave up their children to him, as Abraham gave up his son Isaac, to be obedient and do the will of God.

Many parents make mistakes their children suffer for, but our parents, when they recognized their misstep, sloughed it like a skin, absent the serpent but still a malodorous presence. Like furtive travelers, they swept away evidence of their passage into dark compliance and expected us to remain silent, accept this colossal blunder as the will of God. *"We will never speak of the bad things in The Park. We will focus only on the good things, speak only of the good times."* and so the second indoctrination began. They did not understand their children's experiences in their formative years became the tainted filter through which all following life events would pass.

More than 100 children lived there from its inception until its demise when The Park split, and folks started leaving. Many of us have memories of pleasant events, occasional exhilarating moments, childhood friendships, and terrible memories of fear-based lessons, mental, physical, sexual, and spiritual abuse during our lives there. How can good people be induced to do awful things and how did these people we learned to fear and hate, revert to being the family and friends we love?

It is *"water under the bridge,"* but the children's lives took root in that water, and our tree of life is shaped by it. We moved beyond the borders of The Park, our broken parts tucked away to reveal themselves at the most unexpected times. We've lost some to untimely death, while others choose to live within the church's fundamental premise and raise their children in this way. Still, none of them live to the expectations of The Message, impossible in a millennial world, the advent of technology, digital research, information sharing, television, computers, smartphones, and social media. Things that keep them from *"Applying the Token"* to their household, leaving them unsealed, unsanctified, no different than any of us who have recognized cult doctrine and do not believe The Message is our way to an eternal future.

Though twins, two beings who shared a profound bond from our conception, Esther and I were affected by this experience in different ways. The Park was the only life we knew until age fourteen. We survived our childhood, but latent injury accompanied both of us into adult life. She lived expressively, loved quickly, launched herself impulsively into the music, the crowd, or the conviction of the moment. I became goal-oriented, tightly wound, skeptical of love and trust, full of my own will, or as Esther said, *"All of us are addicted to something Doodle. You are addicted to control."* She was right, whatever the nature of an addiction, it is always driven by imbedded emotion, memorized fear, and trauma.

Esther forgot much of our childhood, but she remembered when she drank. Intoxicated, screaming at God, she emoted elemental fear. She shrank from dark shadows creeping around corners and up through the floors, reaching for her, perpetuating the twist in her mind that she had not lived righteously enough. Her death wrecked me and freed me. My voiceless shell cracked, and I beaked my way out like a damp featherless bird.

According to the credo of my childhood, I am a woman with inferior status, unworthy of podium or audience. Even so, I am committed and I will share what I endured, and how false doctrine altered the course of my life. These simple truths will give pinfeathers to other fledgling birds, eventual wings to fly them from the *"chicken yard"* where they scratch and peck, forever seeking what they received the moment they were born.

CHAPTER 1 – Suffer the Children

Some children are precocious by nature

like limpets
cling to wet rocks
I clung
to the knowledge
of things
heard once
remembered
seen once
internalized
read once
retained

my emerging brain
hellish crucible
embraced
molten memories
cooled
them to
layered steel

excruciating
humiliations
painful
acquiescence
scything
defamations

interpretations
detrimental
to the fundament
of an inquisitive nature
created intense
curiosity, sneaky rebellions

undeniably, they
taught me the
wages of sin
menaced me
with God-fearing
hyperbole
consigned me to
"The Lake of Fire"
beat me
unmercifully
for my sins
sinned
right before
my eyes

I felt
insulted
confused
by this
lack of insight
continuity
integrity
in my abusers

as if
a child
has no
memory
makes no
connections
sees nothing
hears nothing

CHAPTER 2 - Twinning

Esther

the day
and the hour
of your birth
are the same
as mine
our primal hearts
beat in unison
antediluvian
cortex
remembers
my embryonic ally

in utero
we orbited
like two moons
attached to
umbilical bungees
intimately safe
in the watery world
beneath mama's heart
delighted
in the singular
wonder
of our pleural
identity
gelid tadpoles
we wiggled
and watched
growing fingers
and toes
glossy roe eyes
translucent
eyelids

we flexed and
spun in the
mammalian
tranquility of
muffled drums
ethereal primitives
delicate souls not yet
defiled with
plagiarized lies
we sucked pink
Lilliputian thumbs
poked each other
through pulsing
red orchid walls
quotidian
inexorability
squeezed craniums
tiny rib cages
folded extremities

mama, familiar
with progressive
pregnancy, stretch
and push of DNA
mingled humans
habiting her womb
heaviness of an
unbalanced load
far out in front of her
already pushed
ten babies
into a hard world
she went one more time
to the darkness
of intractable pain
possible demise
suffered our ripping
indelicate
breech arrival

footling, I dropped
into the chaos outside
you followed
an unusual
thirty minutes later
as if you
considered
a different existence
the doctor
delivered another
woman's child
between you and I
the last of
mama's babies

daddy held us
each in turn
said he knew right away
"This one is Deborah Ellen
and this one is Esther Helen."
he said, as babies
I always had ahold
of your hand
or some part of you
linked
we existed
rocking
twin babbling
ensconced
in a happy chrysalis
content together

happy toddlers
"Always rocking, rocking, rocking."
in unison, thumping
the back of the couch
into the wall
elicited a secret
burbling conlang

I anchored you
tethered your
heart to mine
you, a watcher
quiet and shy
peeking from behind me
you let me lead
I talked for both of us

pre-adolescent
you suffered
more than I
from inflicted
abuses, your
guileless mind
found outlet
in illness, earaches
stomach aches
nervous vomiting
bed wetting
biting your
fingernails
bloody

teenagers
after The Park
you flamed into
comet fire ferocity
reckless, fearless
running wild
driving too fast
wrecking cars
losing jobs
drinking booze
smoking weed
sneaking out
our windows
in the night
or inviting boys in

inept teenager
I immersed
myself in books
secretly stashed
wishing to be
anything other
than a plain
confused
Caucasian female

Native culture
intrigued me
I braided my hair
wrapped it with
leather and beads
confounded
daddy and mama
wearing headbands
and feathers
listened to whispers
suffered sly glances
from other teens
unable to comprehend
my internal
oddness

I escaped into
mercurial fantasy
constructed an oasis
in the back of my eyes
invigorated
by the slip of them
left to right
eager brain
gulped, absorbed
sublime tales
written accounts
and different truths
new worlds

old customs

dirigibles, bright
and controversial
ballooned in my head
sanctified, me?
justified? not sure
moral, immoral
saintly, corrupt
Godly, good, bad
Christian, non-Christian?

I didn't see shame
like others did
had no judgment for
a jungle dweller
with a tattooed face
and feathers in her ears
bare breasts and
scantily covered pudenda
no desire to save her
with my religion
rather, I yearned
to join her
sit before her fire
learn from her
some tribal allegiance
is no religion a bad thing?
which religion is
all knowing
compassionate?

I worked every day
in my brother-in-law's
Carpet Shop
diligent mind
on future goals
always our anchor
I became the watcher

of your shenanigans
pulling the wool
on daddy and mama
occasionally, I
reeled you in
before total chaos

late teens
our lives diverged
so young, full
of heated urges
you married a man
you barely knew
had a child and
one on the way
by the time
my scheming
prevailed and got
me to college

coercions as children
choices as adults
forgotten memories
forever memories
brittle shards
both mangle
and cut deep
we spent
the majority
of our lives
trying to piece
together
at least a shadow
of the whole

the end of your life
greyish tsunami
crushing tidal force
helped me see

everything
I could have done
differently
I can't go back
pay more attention
give you more time
your last words
a thrumming
echo in my bones
"I love you Doodle."

emulating lost
childhood
I curled around you
twinning once again
laid my head
on the pillow
next to yours
crossed
metaphysical
boundaries
forever oathbound
I will make this right
behind a blurred
azureous veil

I watched your
breath, *sighing*
sighing……. sigh…ing……stop
glimpsed convergence
a bright implosion
earthly entity
and supernova
blindingly
winked out
existence chosen

death eased
the etched furrows

from your brow
hard rictus of pain
from your face
left it smooth
unmarred
cool and beautiful
as yellowed marble

peaceful......

I held your
colorless hand
noted, distantly
bloodless fingernails
at the end
of your life
bitten to the quick

pulverized heart
tripped, faltered
when strange men
zipped you into a
long white bag
meant for other people
never you, reeking
it smelled
like the plastic
baby dolls
from our childhood
with eyes that blinked
and moved

amaranthine tears
fell unheeded
visionless gaze
into future days
without you
I couldn't let you
go *alone*

into refrigerated
darkness
couldn't let
unknown men
walk out the door
with you, solemnly
draped in cobalt
blue velvet, a
silent nonentity on
their squeaky gurney

she's dead…
blitzed around me
eerily unreal
a wavering queasy halo
she's dead…
crashed in my skull
horribly real
a blunted hammer

cancer, creeping
progression
assisted by
pervasive denial
craving thirsts
alcohol and cigarettes
your tonic
for mental
hamster wheel
vexations
all, pushed mind
and body
past endurance
to early terminus

our sisters
devastated
weeping, voiced
soft incredulities

"How could we lose the baby of the family first?"
they held me, allowed
my helplessness
against
this inequity

enkindled to scream
silently, I wailed
numb, I felt you go
sightless, I watched
as the door closed
behind you
deafened, I heard
gravel crunch
in our driveway
as they took you
and slowly
drove away
into the dark night

We buried you a short week later

near daddy and mama
deep in the antelope spotted
grasslands at the foot of
Mingus Mountain

I knew your soul, conflicted self
hidden fears, condemnations
yet, no criticisms voiced, you
expressed devotion easily

lived loudly, carefree, and brash
in a drunken ramble, you shared
"I am just a stinkweed under a pile of shit, but it doesn't matter, the sun can find stinkweeds buried in shit."

acid tears, deeply captive in
a grotto of coalesced grief
fragile iridescent bubble
suspended, no wavering

no leave given, to burst
emotional fragility would rob
strength from my words
ruin deep resolution, intent

I gazed upon people who
questioned, with brow wrinkling
concern, your eternity
the condition of your soul

unable to understand, simple
faith was warped in our becoming
no miracles for us, Jesus did not
show up to save us from

deeply obedient piety, wielded
like a blunt weapon, no

Godly correction unimaginable
in fervent, manipulated minds

provoked, I spoke your eulogy
emoted resounding certitude
hammered into the universe
a vast kinetic wave, lamentations

from the book, language everyone
understood, not one could refute
words from their absolute
scripted step stones to forever

"Oh Lord, thou hast searched me and known me
Thou art acquainted with all of my ways
I cannot hide from thy spirit, nor flee from thy presence
In heaven or in hell, thou art with me
My substance, yet being unperfect, was never hidden from thee
and in thy book, my name is written." Psalms 139

I took no notice of reactions
could not care, breathed fettered
doctrine back into pew dwellers
codependent theologians

so many years later, my heart
is calm, quiet cerebral acceptance
attained, no longer jerking awake
forced to remember you are gone

I am not so much beset with
unexpected venom, inescapable
episodes of grief, primal twin nuclei
sync again, like jubilant tambourines

I have seen your amber home, a spiral
nebulae, radiant epicenter woven with
peacock strands, dynamic, awakened
your brilliant empyrean mandala

you simply preceded me into the
afterworld, cresting the waves ahead
of my barque like a playful dolphin
full of joy, fearless, unburdened

CHAPTER 3 – Southern Origins

Our life began in Pulaski County, Kentucky

deep woods
and rivers
rolling hills
green grass
famous horses
tobacco crops
smoky hard
sour mash whisky
made real
in the stories
daddy and mama
told us of
our beginnings

Somerset
and Nancy
two hillbilly towns
connected
by a bridge
over the
Cumberland River

I only met one
of my grandparents
raw boned
ole Pop Daulton
one of 17 siblings
I was a teen
he was senile
shirt buttoned
crooked
chasing mama
around the kitchen

marginally
Southern Baptist
mostly mean
he beat my daddy
with a bullwhip
when he caught him
in the barn
squirting milk
in the cat's mouth
and not in the bucket

daddy's mama
Minnie Della Hudson
died early
I never heard
much about her
except she was
a match for Pop

mama talked tenderly
of her parents
Pa Hudson, tolerant
kind natured
gentle in expression
never went
anywhere
without holding
her mama's hand

I saw Ma Hudson
when her funeral photo
came in the mail
mama rocked
keened, clutched
it to her heart
hot tears and sorrow
endless, her burden
loss and guilt of
the missing child

abandoned
hearth and home

daddy's mama was a Hudson
mama's daddy was too
their common ancestor
Ranter Hudson
I had no idea, until
my uncle Hollis
laid eyes
on my tall teenage son

"That boy is a Garner if I ever seen one, takes after them in his looks, big ole tall folks. George Garner was Pa Hudsie's real daddy, you know. Why, there's more Hudson's in your daddy's family than your mama's."

simple words
new understanding
I heard mama
worry about
Pa Hudson's birth
occurred
"Out of wedlock."
she feared
he would not
be called as
"Bride of Christ."
this confused me
I thought only
the folks in
The Park were bride

Daddy and mama, both born and raised

in Kentucky
both one of
ten siblings
daddy didn't get
much education
after grade school
but he was intelligent
capable, could run
a stack of numbers
in his head
fast as a calculator

quicksilver
not much
he couldn't do
a natural
with motors
and heavy machinery
he could weld anything
drive anything
fly his own airplane
never ran
from a fight
never waited
for a fight
to come to him

daddy always hit first

loyal to family, he
talked about the love
"Welled up" in his heart
for his brother
near whipped
in a back-alley brawl
he heard a voice
directed him
cautioned him
when to act
when to be still

in defense
of his brother
prompted by
that inner voice
he triumphed
over the offender
"A big ole fella, coulda tore my head off!"

took the offensive
charged like a bull
head butted him
in the belly
knocked the wind
out of him
left him
guppy breathing
on the ground

daddy always hit first

impressionable children
we soaked up
daddy's tales
moonshine liquor
running from
the police
fist fights
gun fights
always a lesson
intended
how God
looked after him
even as an
unruly sinner

in old photos
handsome
square jawed
curly black hair
intense, deep-set eyes
cigarette dangling
from his fingers

grey haired
when Esther and I
were born
I never knew him
without clacking
false teeth
middle aged
wrinkles
horn rimmed
bifocals
a fatty lipoma
the size of
a quail's egg
on his forehead

  daddy said
mama was
"High minded, petted,"
by her parents
and her brothers

mama said
"I was poor, proud, and particular."
inclined to
pretty dresses
red lipstick
high heeled shoes
cute hats, slanted
over one
Irish blue eye
smart and sassy
all woman
"But not the funnin kind!"

strong in faith
raised Nazarene
preternaturally
wiser than daddy
uneducated
but perceptive
kept firmly in her place
by old world tradition
and religion
even still
the deep root
and lifeblood
of our clan

early, mama put away
childish things
and worked hard
suffered the way
childbearing
housewives do
lived with
expectations
of her place
in this life, she
wasted no time
on tears, regrets

she recognized
malfeasance
viscerally
bent like a willow
in the winds
of loss and grief
helplessness
and suppression
ultimately
bowed to the
will of her husband
and religious men

eventually
broken
on the wheel
of male authority
kept in check
mind and will
subverted
with medication
for her nerves

We loved mama's stories

ingenuous reminiscences
of life before The Park

first time she saw daddy
sitting in a tobacco field

curly haired boy and his dog
when she actually met him

bawdy country boy
showed her his matchbox
"Johnny in the Coffin."

later, she spurned him
too tender for him, her family

wasn't rough like his
still, she pined for him

sulked at home, couldn't eat
couldn't sleep, or stop fretting

she discerned a good man
in him, somewhere

her uncle set her straight
"Now Bessie, that boy is fixin to leave town. If you want him, you best do sumthin quick!"

tumultuous emotion
recognized, she made a choice
got her uncle to carry a note

*"Of all the gals you've ever seen
if I'm the one you intend to green
You best get your greenin done
or when you get back, I'll be gone."*

enough to keep him
expectant, looking for work

in Pulaski County, not
much wooing in 1937

young women
closely chaperoned

young men made
honorable intentions known

expectations for
matrimony followed

still teens, yet older
than most marriageable

couples, on their rainy
December wedding day

mama wore a new blue dress
daddy borrowed a Model T car

promptly got it stuck
in the torrential downpour

slogged for miles, mud
up to their knees, found

refuge with some of his kin
spent their wedding night

in a damp basement
new union consummated

on a straw tick mattress
flickering kerosene lamp

their only illumination
came to know mama was

perpetually vexed by that
night, unprepared for carnal

intentions of a rough man
unfamiliar with tender affection

still, emphatically placed, the
monumental cornerstone

for their turbulent
64-year life voyage

along the way a dozen kids
their spouses, grandkids

great grandkids, and
great, great grandkids

generations of family
descended down

their line before
death parted them

They adjusted quickly

to a marriage
not much recognized
in terms of equality
passionate, but
a working
arrangement
he, the boss
earned their keep
she, the vessel
for his seed
domesticated
ready for
procreation

"I loved him but he was a hard, selfish man."

life, became routine
daddy backslid
to his old ways
drinking, fighting
dallying with loose women
mama, hot tempered
and angry, had
chanced at
something better
wondered how
to hit him back

"I was gonna patch his pants with the same cloth."

curled her hair
dressed up in her best
pulled on sheer stockings
high heeled shoes
ruby red lipstick

"I was goin to town, but he stopped me in the door."

daddy ripped her dress
stockings, and shoes
right off, threw
them in the fire
left her bare

"Well, I wasn't the funnin kind anyway."

mostly, mama
tolerated a
situation she
was powerless
to change
kept her temper
until deep into
pregnancy with
their first son

"Pregnant with his child, him sparkin women, I could smell em on him when he come in."

disappointed
fed up, mama
heavily pregnant
stood behind
their door
planned
to smash him
on his head
with her shoe
as he returned

"From runnin the town."

always prescient
he didn't know
it was her, until
he whirled round
punched her
in the jaw daddy always hit first

CHAPTER 4 – The Weight of a Name

Daddy told mama he wanted

a dozen kids, this
desire accomplished
in the first
twenty-three years
of marriage

mama never wanted
more children
after her second
pregnancy
and first set of twins
Margie Ellen died
within hours
Marietta lost
something
indefinable
forever

mama didn't
have many choices
tradition dictated
even this
personal decision
events of the body
carrying babies to term
expectation for
wrenching pain
possible death
lockstep with
parturition trauma

a woman when
women were silent
she stayed
in her home
always pregnant
singular poignant
choice, to love
every baby equally

it was daddy
"Would get to hankerin for another one."
about the time
she weaned
the youngest
he had a thing
about naming all
of his boys with a "J"
when Tony was born
mama named him

daddy, just wise
enough to let it pass
every time
she turned up
pregnant
mama chose happiness
"Wasn't no point in crying over a new baby."
always room
for one more
in her heart

Mama did the work

daddy did the bragging
a thousand times
he spoke
"I have five sons for G-R-A-C-E, and seven daughters for the Seven Church Ages."
he'd tick
them off
on his fingers
"Ephesus, Smyrna, Pergamos, Thyatira, Sardis, Philadelphia, and Laodicea."

named his
first four daughters
before he met
the Prophet
last three, all
Biblical monikers

Sharon Rose
from the lyrical
Song of Solomon
more so
named for
Brother Branham's
daughter who died
as an infant

Esther Helen
named for
the formidable
biblical queen
in Hebrew, *Hadassah*
ancient Persian, *Ishtar*
Spanish, *Estrella*
all mean, *Star*

*Star....i*s that what

you are?
a celestial fire
forced, for a time
to corporeal being
misplaced on
this blue planet
accidentally linked
to life on a ribald
earth world?
ephemeral white dwarf
you burned hot
vivacious and radiant
flickered down
and blazed away

daddy named me
Deborah Ellen
for the only known
female judge
mentioned
in the Bible
in Hebrew, *"Bee"*
buzzing warrior woman
led the armies of Israel
mouth piece and mediator
between Jehovah
and the people
ancient epochal
equivalent to
"Breaking the glass ceiling"

I embrace this
archetypal likeness
my challenge
to change
perspectives
crush expectations

for silence, obedience
submission in women
a doer, a talker
feet firmly planted
in bedrock reality
I do not have
visons for elucidation
I am no soothsayer
or seer of
future pieties

but…I am compelled

to be bold
like Jael
take a hammer
and drive a tent peg
through the temple
of our *Sisera* of silence
pin its head to the ground
so good things
may be done
through the
audacious words
of a woman

CHAPTER 5 - The Great Conversion

Sunday, December 7th, 1941

daddy and mama
in the car with the kids
when they heard
about Pearl Harbor
on the radio
life was lean and hard
they knew
everything
would change
become harder still

1942, running an
old gas station
living in the garage
when Berta was born
deep in the night
they woke to a
screaming infant

desperately
seeking food, the
large voracious rat
found their tender infant
crept into her crib
chewed on the end
of her thumb
naked vanishing
tail noted
"Stinkin thing, the size of a possum!"
daddy, stayed up
nodded off, waiting
to blast it with a shotgun
never saw it

hard resolve intact
he ran a hose
from the car exhaust
into its hidey hole
perfect extinction

they worked hard
scratched a living
from the proceeds
of gasoline sales
simple mechanic work
and country service
folks rung a bell
at the pumps
they'd run outside
fill up the car
wash the windows
check the oil
air all four tires

nourishment
was hard earned
in pennies and nickels
mama's milk dried
up before she
weaned Berta
old enough to
stand in her crib
and wait for her bottle
they all enjoyed a chuckle
watching her
catch that bottle
in both hands
flop backwards
into her crib, gulp
down warm milk

mama told us of
a busy day, everyone
rushing for
that ringing bell
the bottle got
tossed to her
and the lid
was not
screwed on
tightly enough

to avoid the
inevitable draft
daddy took a welding job
in a California shipyard
left mama
and three children
in Kentucky
with her family

working long lonely
hours, far from home
he looked for food
to nourish his soul
1943, he met a man
pivotal to his
immutable repentance
"A fine Baptist preacher."
led him to the Lord
daddy gave his heart
to Jesus Christ
in a *"born again"* experience

he needed to see mama
share effervescent joy
and the fruition
of her prayers
he left his welding job
returned to Kentucky

mama embraced
a new man
on fire for God
witnessing
to anyone willing
to listen, she'd
never seen him cry
until the love of God
softened his heart, he
wept tears of remorse
swore on this new
righteousness
many blissful promises

twenty-six and
married with children
still, drafted almost
immediately
daddy accepted this
as God's will
paid the hard price
placed his life
and family into the
hands of God

"The Army was good for me, got my lungs healthy. I could run for miles when other fellers would get winded and fall out."

destination
Germany
Patton's 3rd Army

"I shipped out with 7,000 troops on the Amsterdam, a ship built to carry 1,200. They packed us in canvas bunks like sardines. 2 feet by 6 feet for every man and their gear, headed out of Scotland. When we was makin the crossing a big storm come up rocked that ship like a little bucket. We learned of a submarine lyin in wait beneath the waves, men were scared and sick, but the Amsterdam did a one-eighty and out run it. 7,000 souls aboard and a torpedo would have put us all to the bottom. I wedged my feet and my shoulders in my bunk and I talked to God. Back in Scotland they put us on a train and

we come on down through England, unloaded in London, where we got back on another boat. I never seen nor heard no more til I got to France and there was bombing and everything else but I went on ahead without fear. A man cain't move if he's afraid. I seen fear get men killed.

I wasn't a killer but I could not be a Conscientious Objector. I thought they were misled. I believed we needed to stop Hitler but I already decided if they put a gun in my hand and expected me to kill another human, I would walk in front of enemy fire and let them take my life. You see, I completely believed no one could take my life unless it was the will of God. When I got to Germany, they heard I was a welder and a mechanic, they placed me in Light Maintenance and Ordinance, but I never told another person my views about killing.

It's a wonder when you're put in war. It's a dangerous place. My name was on the list to go right up to the very front, where the bullets were flyin but I never got called. Sergeant Finnigan hollered at me, 'Daulton, you know why you never had to go out on the tenth run? Cause I took your name off the list!' He reckoned I was more valuable in the mechanic corps so I could keep his jeep runnin, but I know it was the hand of God."

pregnant again
when daddy shipped
out, mama held a
hard space
in desperate
hungry times

challenged with
another mouth to feed
limited food rations
her tiny income, now
near non existent
gasoline rationed as well
prenatal demand sapped
her body of nutrients
and strength
her struggle to
care for their living
children became
more than she

could manage
with some help
she made
arrangements with
a local doctor, assisted
other war wives
to a solution for
this common dilemma

she overlaid feelings
of self-betrayal
soul sickness
abandonment of
core values
loss of maternal
foundation
with desperate necessity
showed up for
a backstreet abortion

she undressed slowly
reluctantly, settled
on a cot
waiting her turn
wounded mind
steeped in the reality
of a deed never
before considered
remorseful tears
spilled over

"I had a weight like a stone in my heart."

assisting nurse
arrived to prep and
position her
for the procedure
she couldn't move

"I couldn't breathe, got lightheaded, thought I might fall out."

paralyzed with
condemnation
loss of comfortable
cultural boundaries

tired, scratching
her own living from
the desperate need
of others, the nurse
placed a creased
work worn hand
on her shoulder
and shook her a little

"Honey, you ain't wantin to do this. Go on home and have your baby. Ain't nothin worth this kind of misery. Just because it seems like the only choice, don't mean it is."

breathing easier
filled with relief
her near miss
a deed to wreck
the quintessential mama

"I couldn't get out fast enough, asked the Lord Jesus to forgive me for even thinkin of it."

unselfishly, mama chose
her unborn child
in spite of daily hardship
lonely struggle of
war wife and mother
she found a well of
determination and
strength to remain
true to her faith
and her family
their fifth baby
Doris Rose

arrived in 1944

eventually exhausted
totally out of resources
running a gas station
and failed tobacco crop
she dressed in her
Sunday best
left the kids
with her parents
walked ten dusty
country miles
for a hard conversation
with the local judge

"I needed him at home"

he'd been transferred
out of Germany
to the Philippines
when his hardship
discharge papers came

"They put me to work building things. I'd welded a bunch of showers together for the troops, made em with old fuel tanks dropped from P38's. I was workin on makin an ice machine when those papers come through. I put down my wrench and picked up my bag. That's how it was them days."

1945, he beat his
last letter home
while he encountered
and outfoxed the enemy
on more than one
occasion, he
returned without
taking a single life
during two years
on the front
war changed daddy

made him harder
in some ways
softer in others
a grateful survivor
daddy credited life and limb
to a God of mercy
he quit his wild ways
never took another drink
refused to take
the Lord's name in vain
stopped runnin
around on mama

took some time
to put down
the cigarettes
but he did that too
"Never picked em back up"
he and mama
attended church
read the Bible
held family devotions
tucked babies into bed
with a prayer
in their ears, and
faith for their future

CHAPTER 6 – Building our Future

Following WWII

fruitful, blessed with
seven more children
daddy, a successful
business man
wealthy, respected
in their rural
community
owned and operated
heavy equipment
bulldozers
dump trucks
tractors, trailers

teenage brothers
worked with him
most days
after school
and weekends
tough but fair, a real
"Throw em in the deep end!"
kind of daddy
but watchful, warned
my brother many times
about falling asleep
atop loads of dirt
and gravel in the
dump trucks

happened
once too often
daddy dumped
him right out
of the truck
with a load of dirt

instant knowledge
imbued, respect for
lethal danger learned

his patriarchal will
always formidable
he reckoned
every one of his children
entered life gifted
with a singular soul
and spirit
each required
different lessons

in this, his instincts
were true, God given
but I never knew
the southern country life
my older siblings enjoyed
raised according
to daddy's will

"God's will"

made my life
much harder

I'm not sure what happened to daddy's will?

raised listening
to tales and accounts
of his deeds
when he was
a young man
a natural leader
seems like
"The Blood of Jesus"
changed that
part of him

daddy's good
intentions
inseminated
my future
when he handed
his life and
ours, into
"The Hands of God"
and became
a follower

nominally Baptist
daddy searched
for the word
of the Lord
in churches
and meetings
all over the
southern states
looking for
enlightenment
and a path
to take
with his family

like any man seeking
he found an answer
in the swelling rise
of a Pentecostal
revival and
the falling
of the Holy Spirit

coal dusted
harbinger
of my future
winged into
the universe
when daddy met
a post WWII evangelist
Reverend William Marrion Branham

"The Prophet of the end times and the Laodicean Church age."

Known as "Brother Branham"

he waged his world war
against sin and
unclean living
preached his own
and many borrowed
sermons, visions
and revelations
to a needy
war torn country

called himself
"A little ole country boy from Kentucky"
down home charisma
and innate ability
to rend your heart
with a sermon

hellfire and damnation
softened with an altar call
he mixed a heady brew
salvation by
the blood of Christ
faith healing, the strait gate
and a very narrow way

"The brother setting right here from Willow Shade, or Somerset, isn't it, Kentucky? Stand up a just a minute, Brother Daulton. There's a Kentucky Baptist preacher with the Holy Ghost."

daddy took us
headlong
into the world
of The Prophet
The Church Ages
Armageddon
Tribulation
The Mark of the Beast

One event pushed daddy forward

unwavering
in his quest
standing
in a prayer line
before
the Prophet
under the anointing
daddy asked for
"One thing"
eternal life, salvation for
his twelve children

"Ed Daulton, sitting here, from down in Kentucky, how many children you got, Ed? Twelve children. Standing right here, he asked for his children. The Holy Spirit was on me, said, give it to him. I said, I give you your children in the name of The Lord Jesus Christ. Every one of them saved and baptized."

I cannot discredit
what daddy
experienced
in that moment
"The Promise"
changed everything
for our family
daddy was known
around the country
"Brother Ed Daulton"
received an
anointed promise
for his children
granted by God
spoken by
The Prophet
"Thus, sayeth the Lord!"

folks sought him out

wanted the same
for their children

Quickly, daddy became a devoted follower of

Brother Branham's ministry
he often invited him
other preachers
and followers
to our place
for quiet
fellowship
to rest and fish
in a tranquil
country setting
"Yesterday, I was down, way down, in southern Kentucky, right on the Tennessee border, and I was setting in a boat, fishing with Brother Daulton."

hours they spent
in their boats
trailing lines
in quiet water
speaking of the Lord
the end of days
and coming tribulation
"The seven angels will sound the seven trumpets to herald the apocalypse, and we will see him in the heavens. "

daddy had no interest
in fishing
he wanted knowledge
understanding
of the things
he was to teach
his children

mama didn't
get much rest
during those visits
nor much fellowship
busy with the
workings of a large

household, country farm
and southern hospitality

always up before dawn
wrapped her hair
under a scarf
tied on an apron
killed and dressed
chicken for frying
mixed and baked
buttermilk biscuits
to sop up country gravy

crisp bacon and fried eggs
new apples sauteed in
freshly churned butter
and cinnamon sugar
hot coffee added to her
wholesome table
set and ready
when they returned
famished after
satiating discourse
with like minds

every day, both consumed
with pressing concern
to get their flock
of children prepared
to heed the signs
withstand the foretelling

"When the sun blushes and hides its face, when the moon turns to blood, stars refuse to shine and fall from the heavens. When the earth has weeped itself into the mountains and deserts. When you see the Son of God coming, you'll shine in the righteousness of Jesus Christ to live forever and forever and forever. You'll stand immortal in his likeness."

this, to be achieved before
the great and terrible

day of the Lord
and the return of
Moses and Elijah
the only two messengers
raptured from the earth

CHAPTER 7 – Choosing the Path

Another evangelist

loomed up amongst
the mushroom crop
of Pentecostal
religious leaders
in the south
a smooth talker
slicked black hair
lapeled jackets
over a clergy collar
shaded glasses
worn perpetually
even when preaching
some of Brother Branham's
healing campaigns
were hosted by
Reverend Jim Jones

Of course, he
believed *he* was
the anointed
Elijah Prophet
but he recognized
Brother Branham's
popularity
his ability to attract
the multitudes
In 1956, Cadle Tabernacle
former home to meetings
for the Ku Klux Klan
hosted their shared
podium alliance
gave his ministry
"Wings of Deliverance"
fledgling flight

the launch needed
for plausibility

together they stood
alongside well
known evangelists
at the center of a
gaggle of Pentecostal
faith healers tied to
the healing campaigns
revivals, and meetings
that surged through
our country like a tidal bore
stirring religious fervor
and absolute conviction
there was no future
nothing in store
for our life on earth
outside of cataclysmic
destruction

eventually
Reverend Jim Jones
founder and leader of
"The People's Temple"
took his followers
and headed to
Jonestown, Guyana
by way of San Francisco
the end of his story
is well known

we escaped
at least
that horrible
duping of innocents

Daddy however, was similarly enthralled

hypnotically captive to the weaving
dance of cobras in a similar basket
Brother Leo Mercier, Brother Gene Goad

religion the piper, revival and power the
influence, sweet winding music raised
scaled heads over the rim, enchanting seekers

dubbed, *"Tape Boys,"* a moniker still used
within the church organization, sold as stick pins
tie tacks, bling for earnest young men

the two of them, alluring sibilant
minions, distributed taped sermons
for the end time religion *"The Message"*

hissed manipulation of prayer cards
the tool used, to get in a prayer line before
the Prophet, more valuable than gold

rumored to be homosexual partners
it has been said, they repented
and upon advice from the Prophet

set out to find good Christian wives
but it was never accepted as fact in those
days of deep fundamental revivalism

this truth might have promoted doubt
in an Elijah Prophet, sent to forerun
the second coming of Jesus Christ

how I wish someone, anyone, had
investigated Brother Leo Mercier
hooded viper, pedophilic powermonger

both of an age with my oldest siblings

Esther and I just seven weeks old
when these two stood as groom's men

at the marriage of my sister, Doris Rose
to Doug Scott, a brother-in-law
I have known my entire life

years later, I saw them, in old black
and white photos, friends, lighthearted
beaming happily, standing together

in those wedding photos, taken in the
old house in Kentucky, before the
hook was set, prior to the reeling in

There he was

Brother Leo Mercier
grinning
handsome
slimmer in those
old photos
Brother Gene Goad
balding, mild looking
wearing
thick glasses
felt surprised
when I saw them
as an infant
I never knew
the two men
my family knew

I experienced
Leo Mercier
as a child
sentient
and able to
understand
paralyzing fear
etched
in my marrow
knowledge of
this bilious perfumed
hell beast, who
pilfered nescience
terrorized
my childhood
a sadistic
pedophilic
monster
the serpent
nurtured by
my family

Brother Leo shared a vision with

daddy and
"The Brothers"
heads of other
large families
he would lead a flock
into the west
to the clean air
of the high desert

they talked of
creating a place
to raise children
in the pure
unadulterated
peace and love
of the Lord

Christian Sanctuary
separate from
the masses
free from
worldly stain
of non-believers
a quieter
departure
from old ways
old homesteads

Brother Leo Mercier
progenitor of
this dream web
spun it around
my daddy
like a nesting spider

daddy, hesitant
to leave the proximity
of the Prophet
though he was pulled
gradually seduced
by the notion, the idea
of going out west
"Pickin oranges in the sun."

Brother Branham
hunted and preached
frequently in Tucson
he bought a home there
and suddenly this great move
seemed reasonable
vision gained impetus
moved daddy to ask
for a blessing

the Prophet
laid hands upon him
"You go on ahead Brother Daulton. I see it all coming out OK."
one line
ineradicable
became the
haunting bond

how many times
did that
utterance
hold my daddy
in place
over the years
that followed?

CHAPTER 8 – The Great Arizona Vision

This epic began the way

many things do
courageous trail blazers
full of faith, hope, and love
a great caravan
of God-fearing folks
picked up
moved across
the country
to Arizona
propelled by a dream
a glowing expectation
for the future
one that did not
include life
in this world
for much longer

daddy and mama
left everything
they knew, gave up
a successful business
disavowed
generations of
old southern family
for a great desire
an obligation
to give their children
something
they never had

Daddy drove a big rig

hauled a blue and white
12 x 60 house trailer
all the way there
in curling letters
on the back end
"Kentuckian"

road exhausted
we halted every night
set the table upright
ate a quick meal
followed by evening prayers
went to sleep in the twilight
a band of country gypsies
stopped in every state
for permits
to drive through
to the next

Joseph and Jerry
young teens
traveled in the big rig
with daddy
Johnny, quick-witted
8-year-old, rode
in the car with
Doug and Doris
heavily pregnant
with their first son
they brought along
their little dog

days of travel
they endured
pervasive odor
reeking dog shit
everyone checked
their shoes at stops
noses employed
sniffing around the car
savvy mutt, pooped
in an open book
flipped it closed
behind him

Tony, six years old
Sharon, almost three
Esther and I
just one year old
1962, early fall
traveling with mama
and Berta, driving
cause mama never
learned how
three babies to feed
and diaper
the large back seat
a makeshift crib

big rig broke down
in Texas, we spent
two weeks on the
side of the road
while daddy
and the boys
rebuilt the engine

we continued
our rag-tag
twenty mile-an-hour
exodus
married children
adult children, teens
tweens, toddlers, babies
and grandchildren

first big stop, Phoenix
daddy banked on
mechanic jobs
or maybe migrant work
picking oranges
Sharon Rose
wrinkled her nose
"It thtinks"
too big, too hot
too scorching dry
too many people and
noisy traffic, surrounded
by desert cacti
prickly strangeness

We moved on
northward
out of the big city
toward the
high mesquite
and pine trees
it was never
our intention
to become part
of an abusive
fear mongering
doomsday cult
but we vested

all power
and control
in the person of
Brother Leo Mercier

It started simply enough

all considered
him to be the
mouthpiece of
the Prophet
treated him
with deferential
reverence
sought the
warmth of
his approval

garnered his
good will
felt blessed
by any request
he made of them
ensured his seat
at the table
served him first
finished his
home first
willingly tithed
a tenth to him

he responded
accordingly
asking
receiving
changing bits
of their lives
one mild decree
at a time

CHAPTER 9 – Settling in

Our new home came to be known as "The Park"

Pine Lawn Trailer Ranch
910 West Gurley Street
Prescott, Arizona 86301

encamped in a circle of granite boulders
and stately pine trees, a rippling creek

running through, warm and tranquil
perfect setting for the gem of our lives

and the genesis of our sacred Utopia
each family made arrangements

with the owner, Mr. Caywood, we could
settle the undeveloped west side

put in our own water and electric
one by one families arrived, traveling

from the sphere of religiosity, influence
created by Brother Branham's teachings

Indiana, Tennessee, North Carolina
Kentucky, Ohio, Illinois, Michigan

elderly women, widows mostly
came looking for security

a safe haven to prepare for the rapture
there was no need for permanence

no time for building houses
burned out trailers came cheap

remodeled, became cozy
folks moved in to wait on the Lord

seek forgiveness, to earnestly pray
and prepare for the great calling away home

"Come that glorious resurrection morning."

Though we were diligently taught

"No man can know the day or the hour"

we knew it would most certainly be
"Between 6 and 9" in the morning

no thought offered to time difference
on the opposite side of the globe

most of my life, even into adulthood
was spent living to the current prediction

first 1977, then 1984, then 1997, then 2000
by then, it was said, we must be

in Jeffersonville, Indiana
to make the rapture

for sure, some of us would be left behind
our songs, immersive chants, instilled

the certainty, it was simply a fact
to try and overcome

"Two shall be together, grinding at the mill
two shall be together, sleeping calm and still
One shall be taken, and the other left behind
Will you be ready when Jesus comes?"

submerged in this culture as a child
always in trouble, I was deeply sure

I would be left behind, this
created frantic sweating dreams

beheld everyone I love, taken, raptured
flying away into the heavens

luminous faces upturned
arms raised in glorious expectation

anxiously sleeping, I struggled to
wake, to reach up, to go with them, panicked

I leapt, grabbed onto a knobby ankle
felt coarse hairs under my hands

thought maybe it was daddy or Jesus
I clutched desperately, looking down

bird's eye view of The Park, I saw every trailer
nestled among the pines and rocks

landscape zipped by below me, clawing
slipping…slipping, I plummeted, left behind!

woke abruptly, heart pounding, breath caught
held, until I could hear daddy and mama

talking quietly in their bed, then
exhaled slowly, like air escaping

from a leaking balloon, still here
on earth, next to Esther, in our bed

sweet, blessed relief

Early days in The Park

a simple and
virtuous adventure
the populous
a pleasing assemblage
of beautiful people
wreathed
in a *"New birth"*
blissfully
imbued with
righteousness

all one in the
Lord Jesus Christ
no drinking
smoking or
taking The Lord's
name in vain
no gosh, golly, or gee's
words too similar
in sound
to God or Jesus

sincere folks
arrived each day
cut off old influences
unbelieving families
improper clothing
television
radios
books
dancing
drinking
smoking
women were
to be obedient
bowed to the will
of their husbands

the head of
the household
all bowed to the will
of Brother Leo

women wore
modest dresses
arms, knees, and legs
always covered
buttoned collars
no hint of cleavage
long, unadorned hair
untouched by scissors
"A Godly woman don't touch a single strand of her hair with scissors."

men dressed
in immaculate
blue jeans
white tee shirts
no ungodly
unmanly short pants
dress shirts on Sundays
hair always cut
combed high and tight
above their ears

only those
dedicated to
the teachings
of the Prophet
were welcome
in our circle
all nurtured the sense
of fulfillment
found in creating
"One heart, one mind, one accord. No law but love, no creed but Christ."

They built the "Tape Room" first

a library for
Brother Branham's
taped, reel to reel
sermons
families were
instructed to donate
their own tapes
until the collection
was complete

pulled in a trailer
remodeled to become
"The Dining Hall"
where the adults
gathered for meals
following that
"The Toddle House"
for the children
to take their meals
a large fenced and
gated mechanic's
workshop on
the north side
"The Garage"

a silver 1960's
Airstream trailer
was set up to become
"The Office"
Brother Leo's
mission control
we learned to
hate The Office
with all the ferocity
a child can create for a dreaded place

Daddy set our trailer

into a clutch of
lichen covered
boulders
surrounded by
tall pines
sharply aromatic
always green

picturesque
and clean
at the top
of one of the
three dirt roads
in and out of
The Park

still had seven kids
at home, needed
more space
several of
the Brothers
built a room
on the side
of our trailer
painstakingly
crafted flagstone
sidewalks
patios, planters

daddy and mama
took the smallest room
in the back
wedged their bed
in with just
enough room
to open the closet
daddy welded together

full size bed frames
constructed bunks
right in the middle
bedroom
the boys stepped
into the window sill
to get on the top bunk

Johnny and Tony
slept on top
Sharon, Esther, and I
slept on the bottom
Joseph and Jerry
got the new room
we all used one
tiny bathroom

we didn't have much
but it was enough
daddy took a job
at the County Garage
fixing diesel motors
fare was plain
life was simple
no phone
no television
no radio
rocking us
before bed
mama crooned
bluegrass gospel
in a soft, sweet warble

"This world is not my home, I'm just a-travelin through
My treasures are laid up somewhere beyond the blue
Angels beckon me from heaven's open door, and
I cain't feel at home in this world anymore"

quiet evenings

after work
needs of the day seen to
daddy entertained us
picked his guitar
and sang in his
twangy southern

"Once in the stillness of the late midnight hour
I felt the presence of The Lord's saving power
I fell on my knees, and I cried to him there
Oh, merciful savior, hear a lost sinner's prayer"

sleepy drift
to recordings
the voice of the Prophet
filled young
semi-conscious minds
this simple security
was the only
home I knew

unaware, in those
very early days
what was coming
separation
subjugation
loss of will
our lives
would be totally
disarranged
overrun by the
dictates of the
still silently
coiled serpent
in our midst

Always comfortable together

content in hillbilly ways, kin
and clan, bonded by blood and faith

daddy and mama had grandchildren
before I was born, they continued

to arrive, Sharon, Esther, and I, raised
alongside our nephews and nieces

rocking babies came naturally
to daddy, he loved gummy grins

baby burps, and giggles, happiest
though, when the little ones

got old enough to stand up in his
hands, he cupped dimpled little feet

in big square hands, fingertips
perpetually grease stained, raised

them joyously, high over his head
like a sweet accolade to God

always matter of fact, never put off by
poopy diapers or teething drools

a seasoned father and grandfather
mama told us once, sleeping with

one of the babies in their bed
daddy woke and sat up on the side of

the bed, smashed flat in the middle of
his back, a poopy, escaped from a diaper

Esther and I had our first birthday
in The Park when we turned two

A precocious child

instinctively, I
took the lead for
Esther and I
stepped in front of her
talked for two
queried for two
twin spoke
my words
back to her
my vocabulary
well developed
if parroted
often, I heard
  "Debbie Dee, ain't bashful, she'll talk to anyone."

a Sister, new
to The Park asked
"Are you one of the Daulton twins?"
essence of
my education
"Ohhh, I'm not a Daulton. I'm a Christian!"
delighted laughter
encouraged
those toddler antics
my own name
was strange to me
our creed
eagerly voiced

this tickled daddy
confirmed he was
on the right path
religion
before family
unwavering faith before children

CHAPTER 10 – Mama, Hearth and Home

We didn't know how sick mama was

essential as air
to her children
and her family
slave to old notions
worked harder than
daddy some days
keeping things spotless
and doing huge
loads of wash
taking care
of everyone else
always up first
down to bed last
no complaining
just doing

the trauma
of 10 pregnancies
two sets of twins
took a repetitive
exacting toll
on her body
her bones, her teeth
and internal organs
after Esther and I
her insides
never got better
female parts collapsed
from their place

our older sisters
helped her pull
a tight girdle up
over her hips and belly
so, she could

stay on her feet
caring for her family

mama got weaker
and sicker
but she kept on
until she fell out
Esther and I just
past two years old
when mama
almost died
sick with awful
infection, raging fevers

there was much prayer
and laying on
of hands
eventually into
the hospital for
medications
hysterectomy
and bladder repair

Doug and Doris
moved to our trailer
with their kids
strict but kind
they set the rules
immediately
if one kid was bad
all the kids
got a whippin
fair enough
with seven kids
and five of them
under five years old
but, our first real
separation from mama
working routine

developed quickly
simple chores
created for each kid
but we played
games too
hide and seek
always lots of crayons
and coloring books
we read devotions
before bed

special mornings
Doris walked us
to stand outside
Sister Margie's trailer
we could see mama
sitting up in bed
behind a wall of
square window panes
sealed behind glass
like a snow globe
shake it and she
might disappear in
a tide of tinkling frost

always expectant
hair brushed back
wearing her house coat
one hand to her mouth
like she was sad
waving with the other
so close, so far away
we puffed kisses
up to her
tried not to cry
we needed her
comfort, but we were
not allowed to
go in and snuggle

feel her arms around us

Brother Leo
made that rule
a battle of wills
developed between
the two of them
he needed to
break mama
she didn't like him
never trusted him
kept a firm wall up
against him
but remained
an obedient wife
followed daddy's lead

The serpent waited and watched patiently

with purpose, like
a heavy bodied, black
and yellow beaded
Gila Monster
forked tongue flicking
poisonous
repulsive
basking in his
warm stone temple
self-deification
growing

waiting
to pounce
on what he
called mama's
"Phileo love"
replace it with
his notion of
God's corrective
"Agape love"

mama's kids
were her life
the dynamic force
she gave her
energy to
she served God
caring for
her children and
the monster knew that

no better way
to break her
than to
remove her
from her
children

Mama recovered but the scare of nearly losing her

created inexplicable clinging need
unable to discern our real fear

of life without her, we dipped deeply
into her well of steadfast devotion

evenings, daddy and mama regaled
us with humorous tales, how she got

mad at him, stomped a hole in the back
of his hand when he was trying

to teach her how to drive a car
that moving mechanical mystery

quick thinking, he punched his hand
down on the brake, just before

she remembered where it was
he said, she had a hot temper

flaming fierce when they were young
"Like a buzz saw runnin backwards."

sometimes frustration kindled that
temper but she snuffed it quickly

overcome with guilt and biblical shame
of the weaker vessel, always a hovering

label, contentious, disobedient wife
displeasing to the Lord, reminded daily

"Submit to your husbands, as to the Lord, for the husband is the head of the wife, even as Christ is the head of the church."

our mama, soft and bosomy, home

where we laid our heads, received sweet

quiet care, lilting memory of her
chapped hands, cracked fingers

brushing soft across my face, tucked
hair behind my ear, fingertip touched

freckles on my nose, softly whispered
"Debbie Dee," and kissed my brow

she smelled like peaches, flour and
grits, just a hint of the bacon grease

she kept in a can, back of the stove, re-used
for frying eggs, corn pones, and potatoes

always tolerant of the passel of kids
and grandkids playing in front of her trailer

recognized ever voracious appetites
and rumbly bellies, always ready with

cold meatloaf on a biscuit, sweet
ice tea, sometimes oatmeal cookies

we soaked up the radiant warmth
of her maternal sun, sheltered

in her mama grizzly protection
before she was subdued, broken

compliant, and we became shuttled
orphans, removed from her

and tightly wrapped into
bondage under a sick maniac

yoked like oxen to a fixed set of religious expectations

Discipline was a matter of

cultural expectations and bible teaching
fundamental elements for a righteous child

"Strike your child with a rod and you deliver his soul from hell. Chasten him while there is hope, and let not thy soul spare for his crying. The rod of discipline imparts wisdom but a child left to himself is foolish, and disgraces his parents."

whippins happened for childish things
little fibs, a messy bedroom, or continued

squabbling after daddy hollered at us
"Y'all stop that Tom foolery!"

we knew what was coming when he sternly
announced, *"Girls, get on in here."*

he'd talk for a while, remind us of rules
his fatherly duties, and why we were

about to get a whippin, stood us front
of the couch, arms up and forward

eyes directed to a large oceanscape in a
gold toned frame; daddy got it for ten dollars

at the Coronet store, it lived in our house
house for years, along with a photo of

the Prophet, Hoffman's head of Christ, and
a small replica of Michelangelo's Moses

incongruously, horned like a goat, daddy
said those were actually rays of light

as whippins commenced daddy counted
out five swats on the butt for each of us

afterward, reached for us with open
arms, *"Now, come hug my neck"*

he pulled us close, squeezed us hard
and tight, *"You know I love you"*

parental lesson registered
unable to resist offered peace

I pressed my face against his
scratchy cheek, laid my fingertips

over the smooth shiny burn scar on
his neck, relic from some old mishap

I inhaled his familiar smell, work sweat
shaving cream, and car grease

emotional wineskin filled to bursting
warm rushing tears flowed from me

cleansed away the scolding and the
whippin, I never got any punishment

from daddy, I could not endure, always
slept hard after a whippin, felt protected

mama left real whippins to daddy
more likely to swat us with a hairbrush

when she was annoyed, and after whippins
she consoled us with hugs and snuggles

sometimes half a stick of cinnamon gum
both knew we needed commitment

and caring attention after discipline
as the father of twelve children

daddy had realistic expectation
for blunders, disobedience

In the moment

documenting
this memory
I felt deep wrenching
sorrow for him
things went awry
when his instincts
got fouled up
with expectations
for preparing
his children
to escape
the coming
apocalypse

I recognized
the unrecognizable

loss of confidence
doubt in himself
his capable
fathering
obliterated in
a black hole
of religious
teachings

CHAPTER 11– The Value of Just Enough

Fridays, daddy came home from work with

a roll of baloney
under one arm
and a brown bag
of goodies
under the other
Fritos, Bean-dip
Coca-Cola
sometimes ice cold
A&W Root Beer
in a frosty gallon jug

always wearing
a clacking grin, he
pulled yummies from
his bag, one by one
daddy sincerely
anticipated and enjoyed
the happiness he
brought to his children
on those special evenings
he'd line up a row
of glasses and
pour exactly
the same
amount in each

such foamy poetry
sweet as candy lane
sarsaparilla
and sassafras
deliciosity
enjoyed with
lopsided baloney
sandwiches

on white bread
with lettuce, tomato
and Miracle Whip
Saturday mornings
came with distinctive
sizzling aromas
bacon and eggs
biscuits and gravy
wafting along
the ceiling
saucing sleepy senses

daddy, in the hall
knuckle thumping
thin paneled walls
"Roll outta there, breakfast is on!"
anticipatory rush
hungry kids
get it quick, no gravy
good as mama's

Sundays always
a quick breakfast
the day devoted to God
and tape services
on weekdays
back to oatmeal
and buttered toast
Johnny liked to eat
his oatmeal on a plate
poured little piles
of sugar all around
the edge, each mouthful
a sweet scoop

daddy and mama
cushioned us
with simple security
and domestic responsibility

no need for riches
or fancy things

why couldn't it
stay the way it was?

I will always remember

simple
little things
our shoestrings
dangling
high above me
I could smell them
like ants in a line
on a hot day
bleached white
cause mama
"Cain't abide dingy shoestrings."

she scrubbed them
in the sink
strung them
up to dry
over the bathtub
curtain rod
the short ones
are mine
hanging next
to Esther's
way over my head
an impossible
distance

our little red shoes
have been
washed as well
I found them
sitting outside
the back door
lined up, perky
as red robins
on a branch
already dry
in the hot

Arizona sun

Sigh......

unable to wait
stepped up
onto the
commode
crouched there
like a toady
stood slowly and
noted the distance
to the opposite
counter

stretched out
a small foot
neatly encased
in a white ankle sock
lace trimmed edge
folded down
stepped gingerly
over to the
opposite counter
stood on stocking feet
reached up
to grab them
dangling
just there

might have
made it
unscathed
if my feet
had been bare
whoosh!
into the tub
curtain rod
curtains

and shoestrings
all in a pile

Smile.......

Warm idyllic days

we played on the patio
and under the willow

in the small grass yard
front of our trailer

mama left the door open
kept watchful eyes on us

late afternoons, daddy
returned from work

backed the car into
a small space, adjacent

to the patio, our happy habit
to run out and meet him

stepping out of the car
he'd tip his hat back, laughing

false teeth clacking, he'd
pick us up, one in each arm

Esther and me squeezed
his head between us

knocked his glasses
crooked off one ear

then, he'd sweep us wide
round....and round

stand us on our feet
to stagger and reel

giggling, to reach up for

another squeezy hug

a bright summer morning
delightful toy from the milkman

crinkly cellophane, wrapped
around fragile balsa wood

rubber bands, and little
red plastic propellers

carefully we notched together
the tiny wooden airplanes

wound the props tight as possible
launched them out into the yard

chased them, wearing a pair of mamas
old nylon stockings pulled over our heads

faces and noses smashed flat, raucous
bandits, when we yanked them off

crackling static electricity, hair stood
straight up, like adolescent chimps

all of this became insignificant fun
when daddy drove up the road

a hundred times we waited on the
stoop, always impatient, I moved

forward, slipped off the bottom step
and landed hard on my butt, the

rear tire of his big car bumped
right over both of my legs

I don't remember any pain

just immediate hubbub

daddy ran around the
back of the car, dropped

onto his knees beside me
hollered for mama, tenderly

he gathered me up into his arms
hands probing my legs for injury

mama fell on her knees beside him
"Lord Jesus, have mercy."

they did what they knew to do
had faith to do, prayed to God for

a miracle, daddy's worried tears
dripped down onto my head

trickled warm and wet into my hair
an achingly permanent anointing

"Oh Lord Jesus, I never meant to hurt my baby. I love my babies. Heavenly Father, we ask for a healing. Please touch my baby, that she won't have broken bones."

I didn't have broken bones, just
deep black tire indentations

across both my legs for days
daddy's anguished words

"I love my babies"

returned years later, on bad days
the sweet oil of forgiveness, when

paradoxically, I had no marks
on the outside, but on the inside

splinters and marbled cracks, threaded
heart and soul, legacy of a survivor

These memories

form and fall
tinkling like
crystalized gems
onto the crags
and shoals
of the ones
more traumatic

the loss of
parental
protection
penetrating
word wounds
unjust beatings
slashing red
and purple blue
belt welts
a night locked
in a dark trailer
soaked in
my own urine
helpless
in the face of
irrepressible
creeping fear
limp bodies of
precious pets
murdered
buried
ironically
under
the wooden
symbol
of our savior

this deeper recall
a bright glimmer
intermittent
in the stygian dark
white hot, intense
and pleasing
remembering
reaching past
old anguish
collecting those
treasured sparkles
shifting them to paper
creates a ripple
across my skin
a frisson of
goose bumps
involuntary shivers
shoot up my spine

fine hair rises
on my arms
and the back of
my neck
my throat
tightens so hard
so painfully
I cannot swallow
tears spring up
to blind my eyes

stunned by
the immediacy
and impact
of this requiem
such sheer
physicality
of emotions
stronger than
ever I felt

in a church
or a prayer line
ferociously

I hold onto
their voices
fading echoes
in my mind
an old woman
now, I just
want to be
their child
again
before
the advent
of God's will

I wonder
what my life
might have been
without
William Branham
The Message
Leo Mercier
The Park

without expectations
for heavenly worth
without
the constant
suppression
of a female child
born with wit
curiosity

CHAPTER 12 – The Prophet Visits The Park

More people arrived

every day
new families
set up homes
became neighbors
their children
like siblings
in an already
large family

older children
enrolled in school
Lincoln Elementary
the closest one
Prescott Junior High
one block past that
high school didn't
matter much
the kids were
never going to go
that far in school

a well established
religious group
by 1964
with rituals
and practices
in place

dedicated to
the teachings
of The Prophet
pleased and proud
when he came to visit
for the first time

May 31, 1964
one of the annals
in the history
of The Park
we prepared
for meetings
in the only
double wide trailer

Brother Branham
arrived and
firmly fixed the place
and its' Godly
directive in
the minds of
the folks living here

a small gathering
anticipatory
preparation
warm reverence
evident even
to very young children
Esther and I
sitting with
daddy and mama
Sister Mary Frances
directed the choir
before the service

"In the upper room with Jesus
Daily there my sins confessing
Begging for his mercy sweet"

a joyful noise
such angelic lilt
sweet female voices
blended to male baritone
emanating

devotion and
humble sincerity

Brother Branham
The Prophet!
a small man
wearing a dark suit
his demeanor
unprepossessing
bald, slight rim of hair
a high forehead
deep set eyes
he began speaking with
quiet conviction
preached a
sermon he called
"*Oddball*"

"Brother Leo, Brother Gene, and pilgrims, I—I deem this one of the grand privileges that I've had, to come here to see for myself what you have here. One time when Brother Leo was making tapes, and I told him that surely there was something greater in life for him than to make tapes. I've longed for that time to be here, wondering? Heard they got a lovely trailer court. They are on one side, the world is on the other, and all you are blessed to be here."

he gestured
to the folks crowded
into the small area
smiling graciously
making eye contact

"I come here this morning and look, this fine little Jerusalem setting out here, little, what I called it, little Goshen. There's just something that wants to hold you. I can see why you people would want to stay here."

a true evangelist
he connected
with the people
praised

the oddness
of our separation
from the rest
of the world

"So, you have to be somebody's fool, so I'd rather be a fool for Christ. See? God said His people were a peculiar people, oddball; a chosen, elected; a royal priesthood. Now, you have to be somebody's nut. You can either be a nut for the world, or a nut for Christ"

honored us, raised
our expectations
endorsed
Brother Leo Mercier
a Godly leader

"I thought, Well, I'll run up and visit Brother Leo and the church up there and the portion of the Body of Christ that's waiting for—for His Coming. How you've separated yourself from the rest the world, and—and come over here to live this way. Even the little creek, you're on this side of Jordan now. You've come over an exodus, a coming out of the world to a place where you can worship God according to the dictates of your conscience."

preaching
his demeanor
changed
hardened, his
voice increased
in volume
and intensity

"In the beginning was the Word, and the Word was with God, and the Word was God. And the Word was made flesh and dwelled among us. Jesus Christ the same yesterday, today, and forever!"

a small child
and restless
mama let me
down off her lap
to walk to daddy
I stumbled

scraped my leg on
cast iron grating
front of the
faux fireplace
that tiny event
and stinging pain
tied the memory
a childish connection
to something external
a deeper impression

the Prophet
thundered on
overarching theme
lowly *women*
iniquitous creation

"They wanted to strip their clothes off of them, these women, wanted to wear shorts and bikinis, or what you call them. They wanted to have a haircut like men, and—and—and do these things and maintain their testimony just the same, these so-called Christians."

listening, silent
weeping women
modestly dressed
internal tempest
suppressed
heads bowed, repentant
striving to overcome
a predicament of birth
he closed with a prayer
and more accolades
assurances to
the men of The Park

"Bless Brother Leo, Brother Gene, Brother Daulton, and all these fine men and their wives. Happy, contented, and to see the smiles! No wonder, our Brother Leo said it's a bit of sunshine. Keep the enemy across the river."

weeks after this visit

The Park basked
in blissful uniqueness
replaying the tape
soaking up blessings
approval, voiced
accolades from the Prophet

Caught in the slip stream

of glorified
emotions
and favorable
vindications
from the Prophet
Brother Leo
claimed
the ermine
mantle
leader king
demi-prophet

presented himself
as the new Elisha
received
prognostic
revelation
and power
double portion
from
the Elijah
Prophet

infused
with enthusiastic
praise from
the Prophet
people of
The Park
absorbed this
accepted it
as fact
allowed
their will
to be usurped
by his ascent
convictions

self-thoughts
personal
discernment
diminished
by fixed
devotion to
the Prophet
and what they
perceived as
God's will
vocalized
to the people

no longer
simply
Brother Leo
he morphed
became a
different entity
"The Servant of The Lord"

One and a half years later

on a Sunday
October 31, 1965
The Prophet
came again
his last visit to
The Park

Halloween
an occasion
never allowed
on our radar
this time
he walked
dirt roads
visited every
trailer home
cleaned
and arranged
to perfection

families
in their best
at full attention
many with
gifts and tithes
awaiting
"Message Royalty"

The Prophet
accompanied
by his retinue
of religious men
those supporting his
revival meetings
pastors, evangelists
alike in garb
dark suits and ties

sycophantic
servile in regard
to the Prophet
loftily reverential
to folks of The Park
stern, dedicated
royal guards
as he made his way
like a Monarch
on progress
among his people

we greeted him
on our patio
he lifted Esther and I
one by one
placed a hand
on Sharon's head
spoke of a righteous
future to our glowing
adulatory
daddy and mama

could he see
what was coming
in the pursuit
of a righteous future?

did this Prophet
see me sitting alone
on a black night
soaked in
my own urine
tattered dress
tear-streaked face
bloody toes
burned fingers
hair yanked
out of my head

immature
mind slipping?

This time the children sang for him

presented a
"Love offering"
saved up
pennies and coins

"Gimme that old time religion!
Gimme that old time religion!
Gimme that old time religion!
It's good enough for me!"

the second sermon
preached
in The Park
he called
"Leadership"
again, kept our lives
in the place
deeply entrenched

"I had the privilege this afternoon to visit your homes. I never seen, walked into any, I'm going to call it a village, that I ever seen so many clean, neat homes and people, and so much respect for Christ and the Gospel. Brother Leo and Gene, who taken me around and visit your homes. You're certainly started on the right road, just keep going and God will be with you."

named Brother Leo
as our shepherd
and devout leader
called by God
to keep us from
going astray

"Brother Leo here, your brother, see, now he had a talent, to come and lead people. We have to be led. You know, God likened us unto sheep. And did you know a sheep can't lead itself? He'll wander away and stray away, and he—he just can't lead himself. And he has to have somebody to lead him."

he spoke to
the children
prayed for us
commended
our calling
to separate from
the things of
the world

"Lord God, today receive these little boys and girls here, in this school of righteousness, here where our brother has come apart into the side of the wilderness here, to bring out the families that desire to separate themselves from the things of the world, to sojourn only for You."

they left
The Park in
long black cars
driving slowly
we lined the road
on two sides
singing

"God be with you till we meet again
By His counsel's guide, uphold you
With his sheep in love enfold you
God be with you till we meet again
Till we meet at Jesus' feet."

a reverent
quiet crescendo
singing men
and women
sweet notes
lifted on
the breeze
orchestral
incandescent
heartfelt devotion
I touched

silvery tears
on mama's face
tears also
on daddy's face
spotting his glasses
they *loved* this man
his teachings
solidly lodged
in the marrow
of their bones

again, that day
every adult
reconfirmed
their path as
well chosen
in separating
from the world
and deciding to
live in this
hallowed place

we couldn't know
on that day
we would
never
see him again

I wonder
if he knew
this Prophet?

Daddy shook us awake

just a few weeks
later *"Kids, git up, come on outside"*
see a great sign
in the night sky

whole family
tumbled out of bed
rumpled sleepy
but caught up
in pulsing excitement
and the unusual thrill
of being outside
after midnight

daddy herded us
out the front door
to the sidewalk
like wooly sheep
urged us to gaze up
into the heavens

dark, dark, night
brilliant stars, live
glittering diamond dust
close and spectral

daddy pointed to the sky
his galvanic emotion
and subsequent awe
prickled my skin
ached in my stomach
"It's a sign from God."

this great portent
for his chosen few
a long streak
of trailing light

across the black sky

not sure what
I was supposed to see
certainly expecting
a heavenly host
of glowing angels
with snow white hair
dressed in long gowns
sounding heraldic
golden trumpets
bedecked with
streamers of
waving silky cloth

comet?
falling star?
mild letdown
daddy said again
"It's a sign from God"
to show us
the end of days
is coming

wasn't supposed
to scare me
but fear rose
like a high tide
in my stomach
and chest
I determined
to stay very close
to daddy and mama
make sure to be
wherever
they were when
the end came

CHAPTER 13-Death of The Prophet

Not quite two months after the Prophet's last visit

December 18, 1965
loud banging
on our door
panicked voices
milling residents
the unthinkable
happened

Brother Branham
and his family
caught in a head-on
car accident
near Friona, Texas
rushed to a hospital
in Amarillo

folks in The Park
went to prayer
fasted for days
a palpable sense of
desperation and loss
enveloped The Park
surely God would not
rob his people
of their Prophet
they believed for
a great healing
he would rise
and walk among us
once more

Brother Branham
died of his injuries
on Christmas eve

his followers
initially shocked
and despairing
fervently regrouped
after the
thunderbolt setback
of his death
deftly deflected
this devastation
into a glorious
new prediction

the Prophet
would raise
from the dead
walk among us
to forerun
the rapture of
the Bride of Christ

people in The Park
wrapped these
wonderous
expectations
in the white wool
of Christianity
even more intently
preparing for
the day of his rising
and the coming
rapture

they did not
believe there
was enough time
left on this earth
to damage
the children
Months came and went

and The Prophet
had not risen
finally, in the spring
of 1966, his body
was buried in
Jeffersonville, Indiana

I wonder if
this is when
Leo Mercier
derailed
no longer
under the
watchful eye
of his mentor

The Park
was forgotten
by the world of
The Message
and like Lucifer
he was thrown
from the
heights of glory
as a one time
acolyte of
the Prophet

leviathan nature
needed a
new fiefdom
released from
its veiled grotto
loosed itself
on the people of The Park

CHAPTER 14 – Cult Life is Established

For the folks in The Park

after months
of waiting
cold reality
in this world
came to sharp focus
the only path
remaining visible
acknowledged
reluctantly
set upon

our choice
to abide in prayer
await the rapture
now secondary
to the needs
of a large group
and growing
children

life required
moving forward
making necessary
decisions
while continuing
our mantra
"If the Lord tarries"

minacious
communal
undercurrent
wormed into
our trailer sanctuary

settling increased
trailers were firmly
affixed, flagstone
sidewalks coiled
round and between
trailer homes
gardens flourished
roses bloomed
along the path
to The Office
quaint, reticulated
permanence
new arrivals decreased
soon stopped
altogether

Brother Leo
appointed his personal
secretary, a small
nervous Sister, with
a mole on her upper lip
her job to take his
personal notes
and letters
manage all of
the bookkeeping
and tithes
monetary dues
submitted to her
in time he dictated to her
the hated lists
those selected
for Godly correction

assigned as
The Park Nurse
a tiny, efficient
woman, hair black
as a raven's wing
a trained LPN
alliance was made with
a local physician
her kitchen
cupboards
quickly stocked
like a regular
pharmacy

Pen V K tablets
Codeine Cough Medication
School Immunizations
Valium
Demerol
Morphine
Enemas
Emetics
Suture materials
Wound care supplies
produced by way
of monetary arrangement

she diagnosed ailments
and treated folks
like a doctor
provided what became
routine injections
for the eventually
opiate addicted
and alcoholic
Servant of The Lord

the Brothers
started a business
Prescott Drywall
quickly gained reputation
as hard workers
and jobs well done
soon landed bigger
government jobs
for HUD housing

with money rolling in
incremental changes
developed
monthly charges
for communal
groceries
assignments
for kitchen duty
weekly menus planned
for The Dining Hall
and The Toddle House
maintenance rosters
for patios, sidewalks
lawns and gardens
many chores
falling to the children

Brother Leo began
to direct devout
servile followers
to oversee
and collect
they quickly
evolved to enforcers
holy henchmen

the type
suborned to it
quickly gained
advantage
over others
enjoyed
their own
ration of power

insidiously, he began
introducing
his own sermons
and recordings
he still used
the Prophet's
sermons
to make points
and maintain the idea
he was preaching
the way of
The Message

we were
well known
in Prescott
"The Jesus Freaks."
in the commune
across the creek

CHAPTER 15 – Tonsillectomies

Our small home never seemed crowded

with nine people
wrinkled sheets
puppy piles
sleepy warmth
shared breath
elbows and knees
overlapped in our beds

someone always
waiting for the bathroom
mama was obsessed
with water waste
we didn't understand
her childhood memory
bucketing water
from the well
for family bathing

boys bathed one by one
girls all together
as a matter of
convenience
being the youngest
with so many
in the house

three little girls
legs on either side
of a wet sister
sitting front to back
slippery knees
bumping sudsy torsos
and elbows
we scooped water

over our heads
with a mason jar

one at a time
mama soaped and
scrubbed our hair
stood us for a
brisk wash with
Ivory soap
crown to soles
squirming giggles
when she scrubbed
between our toes
eyes squeezed shut
heads tipped back
mama rinsed
soapy hair with
a long handled
kitchen pot

out of the tub
wrapped tightly
in a bath towel
this was mama's time
she held us in her lap
for lingering, squeezy
hugs and kisses
followed by
a brisk rub down

carefully, she
brushed tangles
from long wet hair
pulled clean cotton
nighties over
seal sleek heads
we listened
to daddy play
his guitar until

wet hair dried
and mama snugged
us into bed, tucked
blankets under
sleepy chins

a small Formica
topped kitchen table
sat in front of
the sink, surrounded
by six, vinyl covered
chairs, we all
skootched
round for a seat

seems like
JD and Jerry never sat
always on the
way out the door
we ate simple fare
powdered milk
oatmeal
pinto beans
ham hock
cornbread
potatoes
green beans
creamed corn

time passed
quickly, 1966
pushed into 1967
mama took a job
in housekeeping at
Yavapai Community Hospital
Jerry fell in love
and married Wendy
JD was also working
at the hospital

as an orderly
got in some
trouble, went into
the National Guard
eventually to regular Army

the remaining five
of us melded
became completely
entwined
a separate
smaller family
distanced from
older siblings
life at home
either lively
squabbling
or silent
all of us sick at
the same time

Johnny seemed
sicker than
the rest of us
terrible swollen
tonsils, fevers
recurrent illness

Dr Borne called it
"Putrid Strep Throat"
said we all needed
our tonsils out

a total necessity
but a dilemma
daddy and mama
middle aged
parents with
limited income

five tonsillectomies
required before
school started
It would be the
first year of school
for Esther and I

Choices limited, they made a financial plan

with the hospital
hoped to manage
the whole caboodle
all five at once

with help from
an older sister
to drive and
sit with the boys
curiously unafraid
of needles
mama managed
the three youngest
for necessary pre-op
bloodwork
terrified, Esther stayed
safely on mama's lap

I was filled with
tense excitement
we didn't get
to town much
or away from
the daily oneness
of trailer park life
all the folks there
doing the same things
wearing the
same clothes
here, women were
wearing pants
short hair
and even ear bobs
   "The devil's stirrups"
trilling frisson
of fear for them
seeing their blatant

disregard for
the word of God

everywhere I looked
pale yellow and white
shiny surfaces
antiseptic smells
friendly nurses
one held a little cup
right in the commode
for us to pee in

mama helped Esther
extremely anxious
couldn't pee at all
I never stopped
talking, curious
full of questions
peed the cup full
ran it over
urine dripping
off the ungloved
hand of an
amused nurse

Sharon, always reserved
sitting next to mama
went first for
blood work because
she was the oldest
slight squeaking grimace
my turn next
to show Esther
still hiding, trying
to sink into
mama's lap
there was nothing to be afraid of

I felt a burning sting

as the needle
pierced my skin
an open mouth
ouchie grimace
then fascination
watching dark blood
squirt into glass tubes
I finished with
a band-aid
and lolly pop

Esther safely
ensconced, head
tucked under
mama's chin
still afraid, but
sideways eyeing
my candy
mama snugged
her up secure
both arms tight
around her middle

wide rubber band
pulled tight
shiny needle sank
into the middle
of her arm
freckles stood
out on her face
before twisting
shrieking cacophony

white uniforms
swarmed the lab
for this emergency
the broken needle
sticking out of
her arm, like a

miniature harpoon

mesmerized
my eyes locked on
an unforgettable
sight, a ring of
witchy long
lacquered fingernails
ruby red
blush pink
fruity orange
and deep coral
gouging into
baby pale skin
holding the needle
upward to
be snatched out
before it disappeared
into her blood stream

calamity averted
poor Esther, tears
running, hair plastered
to her hot wet face
screaming, struggling
got her blood drawn
the hard way
her and mama
both exhausted
and breathing hard

on the homeward
drive, all quiet
and contemplative
Esther fell asleep
her head heavy
against my side
pre-op accomplished
all five of us had

a date for surgery

so tired from
the excitement
of unusual events
I slept hard
curled against
Esther, always
our two heads on
the same pillow
relived in
vibrant dreams
rings of gleaming
varicolored
hussy fingernails
and matching
lipstick smiles

Early morning on the day

of surgery, fast
approaching dawn
no breakfast
just a short drive
to the hospital
boys nonchalant
Sharon quiet
Esther terrified
we clung to each other
in the back seat
again, the tensile
coiling in my belly
not fear, excitement

I loved the strange
sights and smells
dressed in
a funny gown
that tied in the back
got ready for the
penicillin shot
in my butt cheek
a deep, pulling twinge

the watchful nurse
with a kind voice
and efficient hands
stuck on a band-aid
asked me how it felt
I contemplated seriously
"Like the twinkle of a star!"

both nurses laughing now
effervescent
glowing like angels
in crisp, clean
white uniforms

and shoes
they pushed our beds
close together
Esther and I
held hands through
the metal rails
until they rolled us
into a cold room
with a huge round light
hanging above, like
an alien flying saucer
I heard about those

"See, the world don't know what they are, what the Pentagon calls them, come right down and go like a flash and be gone. You see, we know it's investigating, judgment angels. Let them think what they want to, call it flying saucers, or whatever."

didn't look like an
angel come to visit
looming above
observing all
I could see bits
of my face in
the shiny metal
weird elongated
reflections

Dr Borne
put something
over my nose
looked like
the metal thing
mama uses
to stop up
the kitchen sinks
"Now, count backwards from 100"
sicky sweet fumes
filled my nose
and mouth

ether....

"One hundred, ninety-nine, ninety-eight..."

I woke up
with no memory
curious, I swallowed carefully
felt raw soreness
and new stitches
in the back of my throat
we ate Jell-O and ice cream
in tiny round cups
much as we wanted
and endless fruity
popsicles

magical days
in the hospital
with a sore throat
and stitches
both secondary to
an abundance
of cool treats
and pampering
discharged quickly
due to financial concerns
visiting nurses
came to our house
to check on us
for several days

surprising twist
gratefully accepted
mama, because she
worked at the hospital
never saw a bill
but she worked
even harder

CHAPTER 16 – Bonding of the Five

We spent the last part

of the summer
cooped up
alone in the trailer
healing from surgery
while daddy and mama
went to work

Tony, eleven years old
highly capable
and conscientious
immediately took over
household chores
he seemed to know
without being told
where his help was
needed most
completely unselfish
indigo soul, an
inherent caretaker
and visual thinker
his concepts birthed
from deep thought
and observation
he fixed things
with broken bits and
pieces from other things
toasters, clocks
flashlights, whatever
he had available

with great diligence
he baked a cake
from scratch, for
mama's birthday, just
one day after his, wrote
on the top with a toothpick
"Happy Birthday Mama"
beaming happily
when mama, tears in
her eyes, hugged him
tight, her baby boy

in the mornings
he helped us dress
brushed out long
sleep tangled hair
clipped it neatly
at the temples
with plastic barrettes
he made sure
we ate breakfast
usually, oatmeal and toast
then cleaned up after
we finished eating
he'd start over again
for our lunch

he stood at the sink
washing dishes, quiet
faithful as a monk
moving, working
his belt buckle scraped
the paint off the
cupboard beneath
the kitchen sinks

Johnny, at thirteen
was supposed
to be minding

the bunch of us
coyote wily trickster
and natural outlaw
not the caretaker
Tony was, still
a magical force, born
with a silver tongue
he entertained us
with stories, tales
of cowboys, gunfighters
and always the
great Geronimo

he got a fake mustache
at the Five and Dime
strapped on daddy's
gun belt and pistol
entertained us
acting the outlaw
gunslinger, *whoosh*
quick draw, fan
the hammer, twirl
the gun on his finger
and drop it
back in the holster

he could incite
us to silly actions
which frequently
devolved to
raging fights
between the five of us
sometimes
sides were chosen

with secretive
whispers, he nudged
directed Esther
without hesitation

Whack!
she smashed Tony
on the head with
a huge hardcover
Encyclopedia Britannica
"Education – Evolution"
both bad words
and disavowed reading
along with everything in between
the last one daddy paid for
remnant from a past
encounter with
a traveling salesman

Tony's head sunk
into his shoulders
like a nail pounded
into a new plank
immediate *Chaos!*

Tony and Sharon
both quiet
contemplative
but like teakettles
when slow rolling heat
came to a boil
they blew!

Tony threw a
skinning knife
at Johnny, it flipped
across the room
and stuck in the wall
near his head
with a *thwang!*
followed immediately
by a decorative
wooden bowl
busted in

a million pieces

quiet shock and
freakish awareness
jolted us hard
we recognized
the real possibility
for serious injury
we made a pact
daddy and mama
must never know
about any of this

It was a time of forever bonds

lunches of
grilled cheese
tomato soup
and lopsided cuts
of baloney
always a thick edge
and a thin edge
in my sandwich
long afternoons
filled with
inventive games
and then frantic
cleaning up of
messes made in
the pursuit of
decreased boredom

Johnny devised
a new game
he shoved a sock deep
into the toe
of the other one
made a nice
swinging fob
to hit each other
not dangerous
until Esther turned
it into a freak show
and Johnny got
his own head injury

all of us running
through the
narrow hall
yelling, trading
wild popping swats
some delivered with

male teenage vigor

an extra hard
bruising...*thwap!*
Esther started crying
and let go of
her sock, it rolled
away from her
under the bed
reaching, scrabbling
around, she yanked
her sock out
red faced and
screaming, she
smacked Johnny
in the side of his head

retribution!

Johnny groaned
grabbed his head
his eyes rolled
upward, like
a martyred saint
he flipped off
the end of the bed
onto the floor
silent and still

quiet now
disbelieving
all of us staring
still breathing hard
Sharon, hand
to her mouth
"Is he knocked out?"
no, not quite
just stunned
Esther, when she

reached under the bed
grabbed a large
sock full of marbles
heavy with *"taws"*
and *"ducks"*
stashed there
by the boys
all of us, this time
terrified by the real
injury inflicted

a hushed silence
settled, like the dead calm
in the eye of a hurricane
we tenderly nursed
the goose-egg on
Johnny's head
comforted him, placed
his head on a pillow
with an ice pack
fed him baby aspirin
he never said a word
and likely mama
was too tired
to notice that we
damaged his head

I could not imagine
a day without
Johnny and Tony
Sharon, Esther, and me
no hint yet that
the demon
would rip us apart
couldn't see
the looming future
held separation
from each other

JD and Jerry had moved on, gone from home

leaving the big
room available
Johnny and Tony
stayed in the
middle room
each, finally had
their own bunk
three little girls
growing, but still
young enough
to share one bed
thus, we got
the big room

first night, away
from snug security
of the puppy pen
sleeping on a free
standing bed
not closely
enclosed by walls
a few feet closer to
daddy and mama
we took comfort in
the quiet cadence
of their voices
as they talked
lying in bed

Esther snugged
against my back
her breath warm
on the back of my neck
she and Sharon
already asleep
but I was wary
afraid of the

eyes on the wall
slyly staring
always there
wicked and glinting
long and slanted
an evil imp
just a couple
of lights from
outside, filtered
through gaps
over the curtain rod
but my imagination
made them a
waiting creature

I pulled the covers
over my head
but couldn't keep
myself from
peek a boo
with the blanket
evil eyes stayed
unblinking
looking at me

drifting off, too
tired to maintain
vigilance, I heard
pounding
in my brain, it
seemed far away
a voice yelling
"Daulton are you in there?"

hammering blows
rattled the walls
jerked from
pre-slumber
fully awake again

I rolled out of bed
pounding continued
getting louder

Wham! Wham! Wham!

on the front door
I heard daddy
jump out of bed
run toward the door
"Come on out Daulton, we know you're in there!"

Wham! Wham! Wham!

heard mama's
nervous voice
from their bedroom
"What is it, Ed?"
daddy running
down the hall

I crept to the door
stuck my head
into the hall, shocked
cause, I'd never seen
daddy in his underwear

he opened the door
interrupted the
pounding, no hesitation
grabbed both sides
of the door jamb
kicked out viciously
"Bessie, get my gun!"

came running back
shoulders curved inward
bumping down
the narrow hall

"Bessie!"
all of us awake now
Johnny and Tony
looking outward
pulled their heads in

as daddy charged
back toward the bedroom
he grabbed his
long barreled
revolver from mama
and headed back
to the front
mama frantic
grabbing at him
"Ed, don't shoot anybody!"
daddy breathing
hard and fast
"Bessie, let me go!"

door pounders
jumped in their car
and took off down
the dirt road
spitting gravel
as they sped out
of The Park

ruckus roused
our neighborhood
porch lights flipped
on down the row
of trailers, police
were called from
the phone in
The Dining Hall

police officers
asked daddy what

he was gonna do
with that gun
"Just gonna shoot their tires"
confident that
is exactly what he'd
have done if
rowdy miscreants
hadn't run off

daddy recognized
one of them from a
traffic incident
earlier in the day
young fella got a ticket
now, at his door
with friends, he knew
"That was nothing but trouble"

daddy kicked him
so hard, in the
middle of his chest
he flew *over*
the motorcycle
parked on the patio
rolled right out
into the grass
young and cocky
he underestimated
the old dog bred to conflict
fist fights, and quick
decisive action

daddy always hit first

dustup settled
I went to sleep quickly
no more fear
I knew daddy would
kick the stuffing

out of any evil ole beastie
come for his little girls

if only my faith
had been rewarded

Daddy spent a lot of time at work

but he had a sixth sense, and good timing, he
understood, stir crazy kids need out of the house

Rosie, our snow white, pink eyed pet rabbit, amazingly
fecund, created multitudes of baby bunnies, too many

daddy loaded those bunnies in the trunk of his
big ole, boat sized car, piled us in the back seats

drove way out in the woods, back of Thumb Butte, tall trees
soft ground, covered in a blanket of fragrant pine needles

left us in sitting the car while he turned all those
bunnies loose, they hopped willy nilly, into the woods

"Now, get a move on! Round em up!"

what a chase, Lordy, they were fast! zig zagged away
and darted like rocks from a slingshot, hard to catch

daddy napped in the front seat, hat over his eyes while
we ran wild, whooped, hollered, and happily solved

his dilemma, he returned home with
exhausted kids, minus a few dozen rabbits

daddy slept through most of our adventures
said he learned in the Army, to sleep anywhere

Lynx Lake, a favorite place, respite for all of us
nice shady spot on the bank, swimming for the day

daddy inflated enormous inner tubes from big rigs, tied one end
of a rope round the tubes, the other end round his ankles

we pushed them right out in the lake for hours of
spinning, splashing, we had no life jackets, no fear

daddy laid right down in the dirt, drifted off to sleep
his face calm, his hands folded across his chest

like base relief on the tomb of a noble Knight Templar
missing his sword, but still bearing the cross of

righteousness, no fear that we would drown, he
trusted God and the strength of those ropes

Granite Dells, another favorite place for fun days
enjoyed by the locals, surrounding three

small lakes, north of Prescott, a geological wonder
"Spheroidal weathering" over a gazillion years

formed unusual mountainous lumpy boulders
we kids were loosed on nature, without the

many concerns for injury feared by parents today
we climbed, explored, chased horny toads

and lizards over large rounded formations
and as usual, daddy napped on the heated rocks

Johnny and Tony, braver than us, disappeared
to pop up above us and holler down, waving, once

creeping quiet, they showed us a spotted bobcat
sitting camouflaged in the rocks, tufted ears twitching

when daddy woke, if he couldn't see us, he'd hit the
car horn a few times, universal signal to return

we'd sit in the sun and snack on raw hot dogs, right out of
the package, six pack of warm soda pop meant we all got our own

CHAPTER 17 – A Prickle of Awareness

It started with a special meal

mama was given
the honor
of preparing
dinner for
The Servant of The Lord
an atypical feast
of grilled steak
mashed potatoes
and gravy, green beans
creamed corn, fresh
fragrant cornbread
hot from the oven
mama's banana pudding
and daddy's favorite
black walnut ice cream

kids banished to
our rooms
but all five of us
crammed together
on the top bunk
in the middle room
eyes fastened
on the feast, like
drooling puppies
looking down on
the table through
a set of decorative bars
at the top of the wall
separated the bedroom
from the living room
and the adults
from the kids

cutlery clinked
fellowship dragged on
"There won't be any lefmmmmt!"
Johnny's hand clamped
hard over my mouth
stifling frustration
the delectable
and special fare
disappeared, our hope
for yummy leftovers
now, a dismal
impossibility

Brother Leo, looking
around, noted the
paint scraped off
the cupboards
in front of the
kitchen sinks
quick explanation
offered of Tony's
diligence

my ears perked up
when I heard
Esther and I
mentioned, talking
about our first
year of school
and the evils
of education
coming in
September

mama knew we
were there, looked up
and with a sharp
gesture, shooed
us off to bed
mouthed
"Lights off"
disgruntled
no steak left
no banana pudding
or black walnut
ice cream
oatmeal would
be our next meal

That moment was pivotal for me

I recognized
the deference
daddy paid to
Brother Leo
he had all
the authority
daddy and mama
were directed
and they
obeyed

Esther and I
nearly 6 years old
we'd been
relatively safe
from his
machinations
I had not yet
come into focus
as a target
in the eyes
of this demon
walking among us
disguised as
The Servant of The Lord
couldn't know he was
already
perpetrating his
perversions
on my brothers

Tony was summoned a few days later

a Brother knocked
on our front door
Tony was
to go with him
mama was worried
hands wringing
in her apron
Tony wilted
pale and scared
looked at mama
desperately
moved toward her
stopped, stood
searching
for.... what?

the obedient Brother
took him
by the shoulder
pulled him
out the door
one last
frightened look
back at mama
before his eyes lowered
his head dropped

he returned
moving slowly
face tear streaked
swollen and red
Brother Leo
had him beaten
for the belt buckle
damage done
to the paint
on the cupboards

in front of the
kitchen sinks

I could see mama
was furious
lips tight
face strained
she ran a warm bath
soothed his injuries
tucked him
gently into bed

senses bristled
cognition cracked
my childhood
I had seen
this before
Johnny and Tony
frequently summoned
returned
quietly miserable

I hung on the precipice
of discovery
about to fall into
a crevasse of
irrevocable change
took notice of
the tight mewling
thing in my gut

awakened
life became
less innocent
instruction
in fear began

hard religiosity
for the adults
guidelines must be met
children must be
shown the way
to eternal life
on their own
without stern instruction
foolish offspring
would wander
into the fires of hell

looking, I saw
listening, I heard
everything
late in the night
mama's voice
quiet, strident
angry, beseeching

"He took them to the creek, stripped them naked....and beat them, he shoved creek sand in their mouth and ears…up their nose. He poked sand up in their rectum.... made them run home naked!" It's wrong and wicked what he done, Ed."

inconceivable
words, webbed
in my brain
like fat struggling fleas
rectum?
winkled, blundered
into immature
walls, corners not
seen around
seeking definition
until it fell into place
heavy door
slammed shut
killed the infant
I still harbored inside

mama was unable
to sit quiet for
this violation
sodomy, surely it
could not be
called anything
else, she reacted
"Buzz saw" fashion
marched down to
Brother Leo's trailer
and took him on

Johnny, boldly
curious, followed
hid behind
the rose bushes
bordering the sidewalk
reported back

*"Daddy had to hold mama back! Ole Leo kicked dirt and gravel
at her, mama snarled, kicked it right back at him!"*

Johnny refused
to call him
"Brother Leo"
indoctrination
didn't take hold and
he suffered for it

daddy, cautioned
to get his wife
under control
hauled mama home
resisting, fuming
used intense
quiet placation
reminding her
repeating
the words of

their beloved Prophet

"Go on ahead, Brother Daulton. I see it coming out OK."

prophecies noted
scriptures emphasized
reminders of the promise
"Thus, sayeth the Lord"
their path chosen
with salvation
for their children
the almighty goal

"All are conceived in sin, brought forth in iniquity. Do not withhold correction from a child, for if you beat him with a rod, he will not die."

mama crying
hopeless protests
eventual capitulation
somehow daddy
allowed himself
to believe
these actions were
not really too horrible
kids would
toughen up
become stronger
surviving them

cracked
the barrier
between the
serpent and us

Those early days

Brother Leo
recognized a
formidable foe
in mama's
strong opposition
to his recognized
proclivities
she pursued him
went around daddy
challenged him
daddy, in turn
chastised by
holy henchmen

reflecting now
as an adult
remembering
my own
helplessness
I begin to
understand mama's

in her late 40's
couldn't drive a car
tiny shared income
everything she knew
was in Kentucky
Arizona must
have seemed
like the Sahara
she believed
the Prophet
trusted his words
implicitly, and so
smothered
integral maternal
instincts

how could such
actions be tolerated?

times were
different
nowhere to turn
no sanctuary
for women
and children
cut loose from
the support of
husband, father

longsuffering
became life
we were simply at
the mercy of
those bigger
and stronger

if children survived
persecution
alive and functional
mental wellness
was not a
considered
factor
always the
possibility
of a lesson
in there
somewhere

the one we
learned in spades
never be helpless
or trapped, *never* take
another's word over
your own, *never* count

on anyone for your
life or security

manipulated
enthralled, and
devout, parents of
The Park acted with
blind faith

*"The substance of things hoped for
the evidence of things not seen"*

maintained
through it all
allegiance
to a Prophet
no longer among
the living
the Kingdom of Heaven
firmly fixed as
our destination
Brother Leo
the wise shepherd
leading us
ungently
to those pearly gates

our parents
took this
milk thieving reptile
to their breast
and their displaced
children were left
to suckle the
serpent's tail
malnourished
pubescent bodies
young muscles
and sinew

bruised and
battered
seeking minds
blighted with fear

fresh souls
disarticulated
on a rack of brutality
and confusion
permanently
jumbled
unable to
make sense of
deeds and actions
directly
contradictory
to religious
doctrine, teachings
learned at
the end
of a belt

survival
required
compliance
precocious
noncompliant
kids
suffered more

CHAPTER 18 – Prank Gone Wrong

A Beautiful Arizona Saturday

tempted Esther and I
to sneak over

to the other side
of The Park, there

a small playground
forbidden to us

sinners lived over
there, but we'd

been there before
covertly, with

our brothers, to visit
"The Monster!"

a terrifying length
of shining metal

the tallest slide
I'd ever seen

stomach dropping
thrill, exuberantly

whooshing down
to the bottom

landing on our feet
in the dirt trough

at the end of

of the super slide

should have
recognized the

dickens, in both
brothers, agreed to

take us again, no
begging or bribery

now, I wonder if they
instigated the notion

another rule, girls
in The Park do not wear

pants, inappropriate
ungodly garb

"But my sister, raise up your eyes and look beyond, to him that said, it is an abomination for a woman to put on a garment that pertains to a man."

we took on the
forbidden slide

in summer dresses
cotton undies

and bare legs, feet in
tennis shoes, no socks

right up toward the
azure blue sky

step, step, stepped
sat down carefully

tucked light cotton skirt

under butt and thighs

all that gleaming metal
gets hot in the sun

blam!

shot down the slick
gleaming monster maw

ploughed roughly
into the dirt

skidded to a stop
skirt rucked up

around my hips
scraping pain in

my butt cheeks and
the back of my thighs

hooting!

Johnny and Tony
helped me to my feet

brushed summer dirt
off of my clothes

seems they spent
the morning, rubbing

The Monster, up
and down its length

with waxed paper and
waited, anticipatory glee

boys!

yep, they will be boys
even bonded

as we were, they could
not resist the lure

of a good prank on
unsuspecting little sisters

had to know they'd only
get one good laugh

no second fool, willing to shoot
down the throat of the beast

our daring adventure
ended early, limped

home, mama scowled
irritated, sent them

to pull weeds
washed my scrapes

with Ivory soap
covered them

with Vaseline
carefully ignored

where we had been

CHAPTER 19 – Brutal Lessons

Very near our 6th birthday

we experienced
incandescent
childish pleasure
felt deep, a fluttering
moth in my stomach
our new doggie
so cute, it
almost hurt
big brown eyes
wet black nose
pink tongue
wash of acrid
doggie breath

daddy named
every dog Fritz
as expected, because
the Prophet had
a dog named Fritz

bodacious
brown mutt
unlimited energy
helicopter tail
precious unmolested
adoration from all
but none so enchanted
as Esther and I
exuberant with
unconditional
acceptance and
profound new
devotion

daddy trained him
pushed his nose
in his poops
gave him a swat
set him outside
to yowl like
he was dyin'

nighttime
he dozed on
an old blanket
twitch yelping
days, we romped
in the tiny yard
energetic fetch
pinecones and toys
flashing furry jet
rocketed back
and forth
prize clenched
in his teeth
soft ears
flying behind

simple and
complete affection
between a dog
and children
we needed
nothing
more than
moments in time
unencumbered
with exacting
religious
expectations

a singular pretty
day, sunny bright

when our little
neighbor
came to play
I've never been sure
why Fritz bit her
young doggie nip
there was no blood
but she left crying
the aftermath
a tectonic shift

still in the yard
when they came
sent by
"The Servant of The Lord"
handsome men
in white tee shirts
our neighbors
with parroted directives
"Dog is mean, he will bite again"
said it was because
we, Esther and I
"Teased him and pulled his tail"

mama opened
her mouth to speak
stayed silent
little Fritz
sitting on
his haunches
tail thumping
looking up
panting, waiting
for the throw

what would they do?

smack him
with a rolled up

paper bag, the
way daddy did?
make him howl
run in the corner?
later, we would
make it all better
with snuggles
and treats

a gun, concealed
in the back of
a waistband
no memory
which Brother
grabbed him
by the scruff
shot him in the head

everything changed
in a cracking blast
horrid disbelief
terrible
knowledge
transmuted
eyes to soul
indelible
radical finality

plunging shock
slow motion tilt
grass yard
brilliant day
suddenly shades
of grey and greyer
daylight siphoned
away from
our pseudo
secure existence

reality popped
back, like
an air-filled ball
pushed under water
bobbing, unstable
are we still here?
yes, and unable
to unsee
grisly death
brutal cruelty

our wily puppy
shattered
animated light
in his eyes
dimmed to murk
slid away, lost focus
compact body
became weirdly inert
dynamic bouncing
muscle now
just heavy meat
head lolling, pink
cotton candy tongue
stilled forever
caught in his teeth
as if he'd tried
for one last
connection

how much can
little girls
scream inside?
Esther and I
too young to rage
nothing in
our shocked souls
but quaking
fear, sobbing

endurance

nescience shattered
and a real sense
of terror
deftly instilled
in its place
aberrant firsts
followed
the kind that
took permanent
residence in my mind

first time someone
other than daddy
whipped us
a really bad beating
whanging lashes
dealt with harsh
and deliberate effect
fiery pain unlike any
prior punishment

no discipline
birthed from
parental devotion
this, an order
to be carried out
each strike
meant to inflict
maximum pain
wide, ripping hot
red belt welts
darkened to bruises
striping butt
and legs for days

it was the first time
they cut our hair

additional humiliation
daddy, required by
The Servant of The Lord
to inform mama

no fight left
in mama that day
she wept silently
I saw her shake her
head as if she
was stunned
mouth words I
could not hear
she and Tony
slowly, with great care
brushed out
our long hair
prepared us to
become an
abomination

"Girls and women should have long hair. A Godly woman don't put a scissor to a single strand of her hair. It's an abomination, Bible says so."

using scissors
Brother Carl
the men's barber
whacked our hair off
short, jagged
just below our ears
in so doing
marked us
set us apart
shamed, within
our religious
communal society

crushingly
tangible lesson

a real and
barbarous price
for misstep or
disobedience
daddy and mama
powerless to
prevent this terror
they became
a parental void
replaced with more
ruthless acolytes
we lived in the
same house
with them, just the
same as before
but our sense
of comfort
safety and security
forever gone

I wish I had known then

the difference
in my brain
and Esther's
I know now
pieces of her
never came back
from these
hideous lessons
she developed
night terrors
wet the bed
chewed her
fingernails
until they bled
vomited at any
sign of trouble

I learned
to make bricks
every insult
every new injury
a nice square stone
to fortress the fragile
featherless hatchling
of mind and soul
I aspired to be
her shield
stand in
front of her
tried to keep
her safe
most times
I failed
it got worse
when they separated us

Random punishments increased

birthed
from the ether
of God's voice
or Brother Leo's
auditory
hallucinations
heard in his ears
shown to him
our sins
and our follies

Sharon, Esther, and I
summoned
to his trailer
walked down the
narrow hall
to his bathroom
much finer than ours
all brown
with marbled
countertops

a window, slightly
open above
a brown bathtub
the brown toilet
a toadstool
dwarfed by Brother Leo
sitting, legs wide
to accommodate
his increasing girth
wearing his usual
spotless white
vee necked
tee shirt
reining pulpiteer
ruthlessly rebuked

chose penalty

the three of us
hands tightly
clasped, standing
close together
in his bathroom
challenged
with deeds
spoken to him
by God
said he'd burn
our tongue out
with a red-hot poker
if we lied, the
only fireplace I'd
ever seen in The Park
was not real
without thinking
the words in my mind
popped out
of my mouth
"You don't have a fireplace"
Sharon looked
at me, mouth
open like I
lost my mind

he stood, fast
struck like a snake
slapped me hard
across the face
knocked me
flying, into
the wall cabinet
hit the other side
of my face on
the small round
door knob

he stepped back
calm, unruffled
settled back
on the toilet

I had never
been smacked in
the face before
peculiar blunted
ringing in my ears
injured cheek
didn't feel like mine
pain pulsed along
the bright red
imprint of
his hand on
one side, round
rising bruise
on the other

he asked us if
we made a mess
on our patio while
playing with pinecones?
of course, we
lined them up
made a house with
a kitchen and
bedrooms
now enduring
senseless
punishment
for innocent fun

someone was talking to him
all of us paid
for my impulsive
quip, we carried
written orders for

our beatings
to his secretary
in The Office

she summoned
designated belt
wielder of the day
we waited sitting
on the carpeted floor
not allowed to
sit near each
other or speak
snapped at for fidgeting
while the waiting
filled us with
dreadful
soul sickening
anticipation
but we did not
expect reprieve

hours later
our punisher
strolled in
pulled off his
leather belt
beat us as directed
released us
to walk home
slowly, painfully

mama wept
every time
she slipped
us into a warm
Epsom salts bath
dipped scoops of
warm water over
shoulders and backs

soothed red welts
purple-blue bruises
and old blood
that drifted down
our sides and legs
like oxidized
green copper

We learned quickly to be very afraid

of Brother Leo
The Servant of The Lord
reptilian source
of our suffering
if he laid eyes on us
summons surely
followed
our senses
protected us
before our brains
could catch up

if we smelled his
hand crafted cologne
or heard
the metal tags
hanging on
his dog's collars
there was time to hide

I *hated* his dogs with
enduring vehemence
Weimaraner's
"Prince" and *"Boots"*
smooth, pale grey
canines, slinking along
beside him, weird
pink rimmed
ice water eyes
ghost scary

it wasn't their fault
poor puppies
simply plucked
from a litter and
bonded to the devil

senses triggered
like an early warning
alarm, sometimes we
managed to hide
from him, escape
the whirlwind
of his visions

Esther and I crouched
behind the tire
of a large car
pressed together
like spoons in a drawer
making ourselves as
small as possible
my breath was gone
I sensed only the
tick…. tick…. tick….
of creeping time
frozen, like
terrified rabbits
I was sure his dogs
could hear the
rapid thunder of
twin heart beats

oily black rubber smell
filled my mouth
and nose, when
they clinked by us
and we could
breathe again, free
to scamper home
pull the curtains
lock the door
and hide

Sometimes one of his minions

showed up
at our door
with punishment
already prescribed
before breakfast
Esther and I
were collected
plunked down
in hard metal
folding chairs, me
on Sister Mabel's
patio, Esther
forced to sit on
Sister Betty's patio
a few trailers up
still cool
early morning

ordered not to move off the chair

still slightly shaded
by the awning
mid-morning
heat just beginning
no water, no food

no idea how long I will be sitting here

he has separated us
together, this
could be tolerated
separation makes
this punishment
wretched

obliquely
frustrated

by the sound
of an airplane
I cannot race out
look up to see
agitated and
wiggling
still, I stay sitting

fear binds me here

by mid-afternoon
it is torch hot
scooting to stay
on the still
partially shaded metal
cicadas screeching
tymbals buckle
decibels rise
ear splitting noise
followed by
eerie, on cue
silence

my mouth is so dry, I am so thirsty

squinting up
at the blazing sun
hollow hunger
growling
in my belly
has its
own schedule

I do not expect to be fed

I try to entertain
my seared brain
watching a June bug
lumber along
can't scamper
pick it up
hold the shiny
carapace
in my fingers
enjoy spikey legs
moving
in my hand

where is he going? are there other June bugs nearby?

I count ants
on the heated
sidewalk
but they are
endless, like hunger
they have food
carry much
larger bits
than themselves

they must share it with all the other ants

Sister Mabel
has a tiny garden
several feet
from my chair
I can see
leafy greens
lettuce
radishes
onions
immature corn
sheathed ears
too far away

belly rumbles

mama cooks corn in a big pot

sticks forks
in each end so
we can roll it over
a stick of butter
shake on salt
eagerly enjoy the
delicate, sweet salty
pop, of fresh
yellow kernels
faces and chins
dripping
with butter

don't see any watchers across the way

I can see
Brother Leo's trailer
and I am sure, his
bathroom window
faces this way
too hot even
to sweat, but
hungry enough
to desperately
dash toward food

oh Jesus, please don't let them see me!

frantic pulling
gets me
three little ears
race back to my chair
furtively, rip away
layered green husks
sticky silk strands

gobble chomp
miniscule kernels
suck in the
moisture

how do I hide my disobedience?

troublesome
evidence, shoved
down between
underpinning
and patio

they won't find it there

late afternoon
it's even hotter
no escape now from
the hard metal
and hot sun, the skin
on my arms and legs feels
hot and tight
sounds morph
to rippling cricket
stridulation
signals the
end of daylight

it's getting dark, will I be here all night?

daylight is gone
scared of the dark
unseen creeping things
I know I am crying
but my tears
won't fall
they are all
dried up
whirled away

with the dust devil
in my mind

please mama, come and get me
please mama, please mama
please mama
come
and get
me

CHAPTER 20 – Barbie Doll

The Barbie Doll was the most beautiful toy I'd ever seen

tiny waist, luxurious coiffed golden
hair, spinning sparkling ball gown
teeny tiny high heeled shoes
slipped on gracefully arched feet

how we desperately craved one
but daddy nixed that, viciously
"Them dolls are of the devil, rotten painted eyes, tits pushed up like a French floozy!"
our lust remained unabated, unsatiated

one of the other girls our age had lots of
Barbies, and a clever round case, pink
lined with satin, zippered to carry
beautiful dresses and multicolored shoes

her mama lived in The Park
but her daddy didn't, an oil man
gone a lot, only occasionally returning
home, with strangely exotic things

Indonesian masks, ivory figurines
African batik fabric, a rich mahogany
table shaped like a kidney, and once
a very troublesome little monkey

he wasn't a Message believer
likely, why he didn't object to Barbies
we had regular baby dolls, fed them
with a tiny bottle, like little mommies

we rocked them to sleep, changed
them when they peed their diapers
missing some features, our dollies
brothers got new pocket knives

tried sharp blades on soft plastic
little noses, ears, fingers, and toes
carved right off in satisfying pink curls
Johnny made up for it though, a teenager

he obtained from somewhere out of
the blue, a large green garbage bag
full of used and cast-off toys
we'd all heard of Santa Claus

knew he is really *"Satan's Claws,"*
but that day was a real *"Pagan holiday"*
joyously celebrated
by five hillbilly, trailer trash kids

Bugs Bunny, a pull string made him talk
"What's up doc?" pull it again
"Carrots are divine, get a dozen for a dime!"
an old guitar, squirt guns, a little jewelry box

tiny cups and plates from a tea set, and
ooooh...ooh, there she was, most of a
Barbie Doll, frantically searched every inch
of that green garbage bag, no head

undeterred, we reveled in our incredible
good fortune, wrapped her neck stump with
masking tape, stuck on a baby doll head
missing ears and nose, named her Tirzah

our favorite girl's name, somehow fitting
after seeing the movie *Ben Hur,* one of
the only movies we'd seen in a theater
the other, *The Ten Commandments*

Tirzah, stricken with leprosy in a Roman
prison might have lost her ears and nose
to the dreaded Biblical disease
had she not been healed by the

cleansing blood of the crucifixion
pouring from the wounds
of Christ, our savior, coursing along
with the rain to puddle round her feet

we felt no deprivation, mama gave
us soft rags to cut up and craft clothes
we popped her head off to dress her
tied ribbon sashes around her tiny waist

daddy, unaware of brewing female
disobedience and taciturn rebellion
built for us a small wooden table
crooked, one leg too short, on which

to enjoy appropriate miniature dishes
hellion brothers caught us at tea, dropped
an old suitcase full of rocks right in the middle
of Saturday, smashed our little table to bits

Johnny smirking, *"Daddy cain't build shit with wood."*

CHAPTER 21 – Predicament of Birth

Daddy, raising daughters, took this job seriously

recurrent in our house
lectures on
loose women
indecently dressed
painted up
tempting men
the teachings of
the Prophet
in no way, subtle

"So, if you see a woman all painted up. you just walk up to her and say, howdy do, Miss dog meat"

these sermons
dovetailed
daddy's natural
aversion to
blue or green
eye shadow
said those women
looked sick
like their eyes
went rotten
in their skull, and
the Prophet verified

"We teach against it. Listen, ladies, there was only one woman in the Bible that ever painted herself to meet a man, and that was Jezebel; and God fed her to the dogs. You don't want to be like her."

I imagined
the very worst
the Prophet didn't shy
from graphic

description and
sulfuric hyperbole

it burst from him
saturated with
biblical descriptions
of death
and damnation
for wicked
unrepentant women

taped sermons
delivered with the
misogynistic wrath
of Paul the Apostle
helped daddy
refine a certainty
women
are easily led
by influences
external to
family and church

"There is nothing designed to stoop so low, or be as filthy but a woman. She is a human sexual garbage can, a pollution, where filthy, dirty, ornery, low-down filth is disposed by her. What is she made this way for? For deception. Every sin was ever on earth was caused by a woman. A Woman's place is at home in the kitchen and when she leaves it, she is out of her place."

he was determined
we would not be one
of *those* women
he endorsed salvation
by the grace
of marriage
to a Godly man
otherwise as females
we must own
the first mistake

of creation

"She is not even a creation of God. She is a by-product to tempt, the lowest of all animals God put on earth, women was the devil's instrument in the beginning."

designed by Satan
to beguile men
habituated
early in life
to understand
our real value
rested in
the ability to
serve and
bear children
preferably male
according to the Prophet

"The Bible seldom records a girl's birth. You know that. Women will send more preachers to hell than all the bootleg joints there is in the world. Let a little flapper with a cigarette in the corner of her mouth, and her hair all cutie curled up like that, watch what she'll do."

girls who put a scissor
to their hair
an abomination
females who beautify
themselves
with make up
nail polish
hair dye
short sleeves
scoop neck tops
bikini panties
trousers
open toed shoes
high heels
all destined
for gruesome

ravage by dogs
or eternal agony
to burn forever in
"The Lake of Fire"

recordings played
incessantly
in our house
heated words
sinuous insertions
seeded my brain

"A woman was given beauty, for deception, to deceive. it's a curse to her; that will send her to hell quicker than anything, bobbed-haired women wearing shorts, painted up, dancing with ear bobs hanging down, and short haircuts. They are not worth a good clean bullet to kill them with it, that's right."

earrings, ear bobs
"The devil's stirrups."
visions of Beelzebub
red-horned and wrinkly
sitting on my head
breathing fire
cloven feet hooked
in my earrings
whipping me
like a mule
right into the
flaming pits of hell

daddy's savage words
fulminant, searing
through gritted teeth
"If I ever see you painted that way, I'll sever yer head!"
as we passed
a mannequin
standing in the
JC Pennies
tall and slender

one hand on her hip
the other drifting upward
fixed gaze, under
bright green
eyeshadow
heavy eyeliner
long dark eyelashes

I had no plan
to wear this kind
of green eyeshadow
totally inured to
seething diatribe
from daddy
constantly primed with
inflammatory fear
of a bungled
eternal destination

I understood
daddy loved us
also, I was certain
he considered
death to be the
better option than
any of these actions
dead, I would be sealed
sanctified, delivered in
a box, to my heavenly home

"God gave me promise for your salvation. You will come in feet first if that is what it takes."

therefore, he put
aside his mantle
of protection
and gave me up
to the man he believed
would help me get there

Brother Leo Mercier didn't kill me

in those years of
spiritual, mental, and
physical abuse
inflicted for
the purpose of
saving my soul

as a child
I might have
wished for death
had I believed
it to be a safe haven
but I was already
conditioned
like *Pavlov's* dogs
to believe
death is about
The Lake of Fire
greater torture
than any
I might have
already experienced

I see and feel
my broken parts
understand my bent brain
my tendency
to black and white
concepts, quirky habits
developed defensively
I feel sympathy
but I have noted
losses did not
wound me

profoundly
as others
until I lost Esther

CHAPTER 22 – Widows of The Park

Living in her own little pink and white trailer, Sister Katie

was older even, than
a twisted, high

desert juniper, aged
similarly, in a vortex

of her own making
scrawny wattled neck

snow white hair
under a gossamer net

as if it might escape
in a breeze, like dandelion

wisps, sweet old lady
scent, lavender water

pink dress, white
crocheted sweater

bent over, walked
slowly with a cane

came to The Park
a widow with some

money from her late
husband, likely not

much, but enough to
keep an old widow

comfortable, in a

modest trailer, out

of the weather, safe
in righteous faith

safe in body, living
with the chosen ones

awaiting a rapture of
the faithful Bride of Christ

she never saw the
glissading demon

until he was on her
The Servant of the Lord

demanded her small fund
beat her with a switch

from one of the
willow trees

on her old lady legs
and butt, felt, I'm sure

through old lady
stockings and dress

in sad cadence with
old lady humiliation

gross betrayal of
simple old lady faith

greedy, bilious toad
got her tiny fund

no doubt with

heavy handed help

from sycophantic
followers, henchmen

moved her out of her
sweet old lady trailer

to reside in the spare
bedroom of another

pious worshipper, willing
to obey the dictates

of the growing, coiling
constrictor in our haven

for Sister Katy, sweet death
her eventual escape

Sister Hattie lived in the small

trailer, right next
door to ours

another widow
short and round

spectacles perched
on her perfectly

round nose
squinting, she'd

furrow her brow
tilt her head

back, so she could
see through them

gave her a look
like a disgruntled owl

fluffy and rotund
in homespun and apron

my oldest brother's
mother-in- law

made the best
biscuits in the world

yeasty, yummy, old
country gastronomy

flour coating her
apron and hands

she'd roll out the supple
dough, shape them with

an old donut cutter, she
left the middle hole in

baked along with the
large delicious biscuit

almost nothing like
the fragrance of

baking bread
wafting from her

kitchen, drifting along
tickling olfactory

senses, drew kids
like shards of iron filings

to a lodestone
waiting, an expectant

group, on her patio
noses twitching

served up with
fresh butter and jam

lard, the scrumptious
secret of those biscuits

never thought of her
as fierce, until she

challenged the scaled
demon, in her doorway

disagreement about her
granddaughter, my niece

The Servant of the Lord
and Sister Hattie's daughter

my sister-in-law, ordered
to deliver a stinging

slap, across her mother's
calm, accepting face

slimy demon moved
to step in through

her door, but that
canny old widow

too quick for him
placed her Bible on

the door mat, said
brave as Zeus
"Go ahead, step over the word of God, if you intend, to walk through my door."

the serpent chose
to wriggle back

into his reptilian
abode, molt to

newer, larger
leviathan fiend

Sister Hattie, left
The Park on a bus

after that, I never
saw her again

heard she went
back to Kentucky

lived through the
kindness of friends

in a spare travel
trailer, years later

she died, her heart
failed, broken, but I

remembered fondly, a little
round wrathful granny

spat in the face of a
self-righteous sidewinder

backed him, slithering
out of her habitat

CHAPTER 23 - Book Burning

September 1967, Esther and I started 1ˢᵗ grade at Lincoln Elementary School

we walked
the half mile
in a group of
other kids from
The Park
two rows
youngest to
oldest, assigned
Sisters walked
with us

bright, new
patent leather shoes
pink for Esther
blue for me
couldn't keep
my eyes off
shiny blue toes
emerging
clickety, click
just beyond the
hem of my skirt
my hair, still short
but brushed back with
pink Dippity-do
barely clipped
with barrettes

always tight
on money
mama managed
somehow
to purchase

our first
school supplies
at the Yellow Front
crisp new
boxes of crayons
all perfectly
shaped, sharpened
small primers
of lined paper
new yellow
Ticonderoga pencils
more than one
for each of us
soft pink erasers

orange and white
tubs of Elmer's
school paste
triggered an
olfactory sense
it smelled *thick*
peculiar, floury
addictive, like biscuits

large, elongated
chalkboards at the
front of the class
the whole alphabet
large letters
and small
on parade above

below the chalkboard
all the way
around the room
bookcases
rows of brightly
descriptive books
mountains

of colored
construction paper
my own wooden
desk with a lift top
an organized
square room
new adventure
immediately
besotted

reading made
complete sense
words popped
off the page
mapped new
exciting courses
in my brain
never enough

burned through
Curious George
Johnny Appleseed
Jack and The Beanstalk
Mother Goose
and my favorite
The Jungle Book

a little boy living
without constraint
religious teaching
or beatings
raised by wild
jungle wolves
naked like a
frog, *"Mowgli"*
somehow, they
dressed him
little boy loins
wrapped in cloth

nights awake
wondering how?

abstract concept
deconstructed
mentally
stories of
my childhood
couched in concrete
"Absolute truth"
word of God

Revelations
our horror stories
sun black as sackcloth
moon turns to blood
four horsemen
of the apocalypse ride out
white horse, conqueror
red horse, war and blood shed
black horse, famine and plague
last, when the pale rider
gallops the land
death follows in his wake
all, the makings of
prepubescent
stress, anxiety

now, here in
storybook world
goggle-eyed
introduction to
things unreal
imagined
and enchanting
laced my brain with
twirling ribbons
word power
and temporary

freedom
from fear
and tribulation

Esther, sick a lot that year

screaming pain
from ear infections
mama dripped
warm oil in
her ears before bed
waking, gooey
yellow earwax
stuck her face
and hair to
our pillow
anxious
tears every
morning before
school, mama
pushed her
out the door

she didn't like
to read, couldn't
make sense of
the words
so, I read to her
which comforted
both of us
they held her back
the next year, some
argument from mama
she didn't want
us separated, but
Brother Leo
as always
made it so

Talkative and full of imagination

the kind that
got me in
trouble at home
I could hardly
contain
my bubbling
excitement
on library days

I checked out
a bright pink
book *"Little Witch"*
a girl witch, my age
pointy hat and a cape
riding a broom, *"Minx"*
snuck away from
the witchy place
went to school
she had adventures
with mortal classmates
and creative teachers
I loved it, but
should never have
taken it home

I read it to Esther
and Sharon read it
too, daddy found it
while he was
inspecting
the military corners
on our bedmaking
and he *erupted*
like a dormant
but hot
rumbling volcano

he *thundered*
about the evils
of witchcraft
said he was
gonna take us
out of the school
that put this book
in the hands
of a Christian child
this was not
"edifying" reading
good only for
those already
headed for
The Lake of Fire

I grabbed onto
that word
"edifying"
it tripped around
my brain through
the rage that
followed
edifying… edifying… edifying
mama stayed silent
we girls rattled
and scared,
had never seen
him this furious

daddy gave us
the worst whippin
we ever got
from him, and
no hug afterward
he, so deeply
disturbed by
our deed
later, still fuming

he walked us to
a garbage barrel
burnt that book
without a
whit of concern
it being a
library book
felt he done
the world a favor
getting it out
of circulation

thought that night
would never end
daddy parked
us on the couch
played a tape
late into the night
the Prophet
howled, cried
ranted about
evil witches

"Them old witches, long fingered, painted fingernails, throw spells on you, poor mother on her knees, and she would cry, oh don't take my baby! don't take my baby! Them old witches take cunning little baby boys, take them by their feet bash their heads up against the wall and kill them, threw them to the crocodiles, what a time they were having,"

we went to
school next
morning
heavy eyed
but well aware
of reading
expectations

I started hiding
books from
daddy that day

There is nothing so horrifying

to puritanical
Christians as
witches, cats, serpents
cursed creatures
with a psychic bond
to the devil
boys in The Park
once hung a
burlap sack full
of cats from a tree
shot it full of arrows
snakes were killed
anytime they
were seen

I'm sure outside
The Park
folks wondered
when their cats
went missing
bright, blessed
people so sure
of inherent evil
in an innocent
creature
never recognized
the serpent
growing
slithering, coiling
in our midst

I read until I got sick with racking headaches

forced to put
my book down
when pain and nausea
made it impossible
to keep reading

my teacher noted
how closely
I held my books
found me squinting
at the chalkboard
routine visual exam
done at school
revealed my vision
was poor, I needed
eye glasses

Doctor Rummel
was the very first
eye doctor in Prescott
after school
mama met me
at the corner of
Gurley and Grove
in front of the
Rexall Drug Store
we walked to
his office

he was kind
and funny, he
chuckled
when I called him
Doctor Rummage
promised me
soon, I would
have a pair of

eyeglasses, made
especially for me
went back
a few weeks later
for my glasses
warmed, oddly
in a box of hot sand
bent and fitted
to cup my ears
and sit on my nose
I understood
immediately
how this would
change things

after a few days
of stepping carefully
while I adjusted
life was wonderful
punctuated in crisp
new detail
I learned quickly
to put them
on the minute
I woke up
place the world
in perspective

reading was
wonderful, I
could read for hours
without fatigue
or headache
but no one ever
took me back to
the doctor
I would still be

wearing those
6-year-old
glasses in
junior high

CHAPTER 24 – Blinders

All the kids knew about the wicked witch

in the haunted shanty cottage
just outside The Park

a tale started by the
older children, passed

on to the younger, in the
way of children everywhere

typical for savagely
controlled environment

no talking, no looking
around going to school

just walking in step
trying not to be

curious children
walking past a

scraggly little house
with a pitched roof

and dark shutters
on the way to school

one of the little boys
at the front of the group

could not contain
himself, *"It's where the witch lives!"*

several walking children

caught up in his excitement

stopped the line, turned
eyes wide, expectant

looking for a warty hint
of wickedness, maybe

a black cat creeping
or a cauldron on the stoop

oily smoke from the
cracked stone chimney

rippling disappointment
no warty witch, no smoke

no cats, Sisters restored order
quickly, we marched on

next morning before
school, that little boy

and several others
culled out to be fitted

with a set of blinders
square pieces of cardboard

settled over their heads
harnessed up like pack mules

they walked lock step, could
see neither right nor left

CHAPTER 25 – Biggest Snow Fall in Prescott History

A rare thing in Arizona, December 1967, over 10 days, 72 inches of snow

three sisters wakened
to a muted world
of glistening grandeur
before I ever
heard of faeries
I saw their bevies
sparkling white
no two alike
spin drifting down
to blanket all
in soft frosted wool

pixie wizardry
in these silent
moments, as if
nothing existed at
all, beneath
drifting flakes
and weight of snow

I wondered if
I stood just right
surrounded in
a world of white
never moving
just, silently wait
could I, a solid
bumpkin shaver
effervesce, ascend
to snowy fernlike
fairy flake?

might I find myself
in some winding swirl

a mystical wintry
changeling, I'd
flit and tumble on
hexagonally
unique wings
settle softly
with quiet intent
exist for a moment
outside my ken?

nope..........

my creaky world
always present
house trailers
parked cars
garbage cans, all
illusorily vanished
under a soft
white shroud

in the summer
the huge walnut trees
capriciously noisy
and full of cicadas
now ghostly quiet
exoskeletons molted
from cicada nymphs
left behind in the
branches, frozen
pellucid limbo

rude reality broke
the eerie calm
like a deep sneeze
the *"whoomphing"*
crash of the neighbor's
awning collapsed on
the car beneath

three sisters begged
to go out and play
bundled in layers
mama gave us
a pot lid for a sled
socks for gloves
garbage bags
and masking tape for boots
totally unprepared
for so much snow

fluffy snowballs
carrot nosed snowmen
nullifidian snow angels
wings in stasis
socks not so great
for opposable thumbs
we soon realized
piles and piles of snow
are only so much fun
when noses and digits
became frosty and numb

three sisters stood
shivering, quaking
while mama soothed
red cheeks, runny noses
and frozen fingers
with warm towels
heated in the oven
thawing, we endured
prickling painful resurge
of fast pumping blood

wet socks empty
of hands and feet
dumped like
large white pupae
on the cracked linoleum

in front of the door
mama pulled discarded
garbage bags over
her house shoes
stepped outside
to gather clean snow
in her big mixing bowl
she sacrificed milk
and lots of sugar
then whisked in vanilla
before it melted
mama made monumental
snow ice cream
a brand spankin new
experience
for three sisters
raised in Arizona

always work
no matter the weather
and our brothers were free
to make some money
hired to pushed dangerous
weight off of awnings
mama, not so worried
about a slip or fall
as she watched them
walked up steps
cut right into
hard packed
snow drifts, almost
high as the roofs

for three sisters
there is laundry, we
shuffled behind mama
carrying plastic baskets
metal hangers
wash powder and

"Mr. Stewarts Bluing"
for the dingy whites
of daddy's grease
stained tee shirts
and gross, stinky
teen boy socks
we walked a winding path
to the wash house
cut through walls of snow
higher than our heads
we watched
trickling melt water
twinkle in rivulets
and runnels

The Servant of the Lord
not so inclined to
venture out
ensconced at home
with his dogs
meals, messages
delivered to him
mountains of snow
between him and us
seems God is
quiet as the snow
did not speak to him
or show him our sins
for several weeks
we enjoyed
unmonitored fun

CHAPTER 26 – Lost Innocence

The summer of 1968 they hauled in

an old trailer
completely stripped
and remodeled it
to become *"The Chapel"*
for the children
they cut in tall
narrow windows
of hard plexiglass
in rainbow colors
arrayed along
the entire length
on both sides
they filtered in
streams of lambent
multihued light

slightly raised
platform in front
a large flat
granite stone
stood upright
for an altar
ethereally enhanced
with verdant
gold and amber
metallic paint

tables could
be set down
the entire length
for summer
education
easily removed

to set chairs in rows
facing the altar
for Sunday school

On a very special summer day

The Servant of the Lord
came personally
to teach a lesson
priest like, exuding
benevolence, on a
draped table before him
like consecrated Eucharist
a large glass of water
and two brown dropper bottles
carefully, he dropped
"The color of sin"
into the glass of water
stained it dark red
real magic happened
from the second bottle
with a flourish, he
dropped clear liquid
into the red water
intoned solemnly
"This is the blood of Jesus"
in a spectral swirl
of red tendrils
all color vanished

"This is how the blood of Jesus will cleanse your heart when you pray and ask forgiveness of your sins. You will be pure and clean again, just like the water. You will receive the Holy Ghost."

neon harpy in my head
this should be the
other way around, surely the
blood of Jesus is red?
dinky discrepancy, eclipsed
by the small wooden
stamp, blotted in red ink
pressed to the back of
his hand, presented

it for all to see the
bright capital letters

HOLY GHOST

Brother Leo invited us
to come sit in his lap
said he would pray
with each of us, ask
forgiveness for our sins
any confession heard
held between him and Jesus
absolution achieved, we would be
blessed with the holy spirit
earn the red stamped
HOLY GHOST
eager children
gathered round
the stone altar to pray
Brother Leo took a chair
on the platform

praying, watching as
other kids sat in his lap
one at a time
Sharon and Esther
both talked in his ear
nodding, sniffling
slid from his lap
stood between his legs
received a stamp on the back
of their hand, blood red
HOLY GHOST
eager for my turn
but found it to be
incredibly alien, sitting
in Brother Leo's lap
this man I feared

he seemed kinda
nice that day
smiled, spoke softly
wrapped large
male arms around me
I had never been
this close to him
 his familiar cologne
invaded my nose
a deep trigger
he placed
his fingers on
my chin, turned
my face to his ear

much…too……close
to his wide brown
pock marked face
his ear a fleshy
brown auricle
surrounded by
neatly pomaded
black hair
acutely uncomfortable
I pulled away
confused by my feelings
revulsion
uncertainty
creeping fear

sibilated voice
reeking cinnamon
breath, asked me to
confess my sins
I sucked in a
deep breath
gushed out the truth
I stole a dime
from mama's

change purse for
the ice cream truck

"Yes, Jesus will forgive you for that, what else?"

what else?
discomfort
itchy niggle
there's more?
I hesitated, thinking
and sat silently
oily voice continued in my ear
"Have you ever touched your brother's privates?"
recoil…head full of white noise
   "Have you ever touched your brother's privates?"

immediately frightened
full of nervous
heart palpitating panic
and leaden
stomachache
this novel experience
had gone terribly wrong
I knew what
privates were, but
I had never seen
my brothers naked
never even in
their underwear

"Have you ever put your mouth on your brother's privates, have they touched yours?"

fear crested
like an unruly wave
trouble!
for me and
my brothers
what do I say?
fresh rushing tears

excitement for
the red ink stamp
deliquesced
to a puddle
of wriggling dread
squirming, I
needed to get away
but his arms
tightened around me
what did my sisters say?
again, shocking
unimaginable words
"Have you ever sucked your brother's privates in your mouth? Have your brothers put their mouth on your privates?"

word salad
confused agitation
growing fast
what…. what…. put my mouth on their…. what…...?
easy denial
"No…never, never, yuck!"

what did my sisters say?

hollow, my insides
disappeared
tiny vanishing point
only my body left
in imminent trouble
and overwhelmed

in a slimy blight
gone, all nescient
desire to be cleansed
by the blood of Jesus
the red ink stamped
HOLY GHOST novelty
no longer important

tremulous *"No....no......no"*
shook my head
clanging bell tower
between my ears
I could not get away
from hideous
oily suggestions
"You must tell me. God has spoken to me and he has shown me the nasty things you have done with your brothers. We will pray together. You will be pure and clean as driven snow. Jesus is here, you will receive the Holy Ghost."

I blurted again *"No... no..."*
shook my head
vehemently this time
bleak confusion
troubling my thoughts

if Jesus is here, why won't he help me?

abruptly pushed
from his lap
other kids noted
something amiss
instructed to go outside
and sit on the steps
of The Chapel and wait
I bolted, relieved
to be free
away from him
his sickening words

still sitting when
prayer meeting ended
beaming kids filed out
all sporting a
bright red stamp
on the back
of their hand
HOLY GHOST

Sharon and
Esther too

what did they tell him?

Twenty-five years later

I asked my sisters
what they
told him
during that
prayer meeting
they agreed
said yes, to all
even when he
asked the
nasty stuff
Why?

*"Because we weren't stupid, that's why! You never knew when to keep your mouth shut.
We were safe because we agreed with anything he said. You were the
only one who didn't get that!"*

I never thought
to agree with him
none of us recognized
what he wanted
some aberrant
sexual satisfaction?
the ruin of sweet innocence
perched on his privates?
I paid hard over
the next
several years

anfractuous path
began that deeply
embedded day
immature brain
a fragile thing
tested mine
to its very limits
his goal, to offset
his deviance

and prove mine

I wasn't inherently sneaky
but I learned to be
I became a liar
unwittingly
helped him
lied about
everything
simplest things
lies just fell
from my mouth
like lost feathers

I was to hear
the word
"Privates"
many, many
times in the
coming days
months, years
I hate that word
with fulminant
intensity
just a word
triggers
abhorrence
remembered shame

I know, rationally
this stems from
hyperactivity in
my amygdala
an emotional
response
to traumatic
memories
creates synaptic
simmering fury

because
the very word
means
secret, mine, no one else's

Following the prayer meeting

I was taken from
daddy and mama
sent to the home
of Brother Leo's
brother-in-law

there for a few days
when one of
my older sisters
accompanied
by one of the
old widows, a
retired nurse
arrived, told me
I was to be
"Checked for worms"

seven years old
I understood well
consequence
of resistance
placed on a bed
dress pushed up
round my waist
panties pulled off
strange vulnerable feeling
air and eyes on parts
supposed to be covered
stranger still
to be frog legged
feel cold invasive
prod of fingers
pulling my *private*
girl parts open
to inspect me for worms
red hot blood
thumped in my face

muffled my ears
shame and humiliation
filled me like silent popcorn
pressurized, my skull
ran out of room
no safe place in my mind
for this invasion

Brother Leo's words
plundered
my whinging brain
"Have you ever let your brothers touch your privates?"

another irrational
flood of shame
and connection
That's why.... What is she looking for?
and, gritting frustration
they faked me
"Checking for worms"
their reason
for this violation

my older sister
stood back
against the wall
silent as death
the old woman
prodded and
poked until she
was satisfied
with her findings
finally allowed me
to put my panties
back on
and they left
without a word
relief, covered again
tiny security restored

but not for long

summoned....
to The Dining Hall
Brother Leo sat
the reigning pasha
in his big chair
turned me around
on the top step
looking out on
adults, still eating
in preacher mode
he loudly announced

"She has been examined and found to be corrupted. God has spoken to me, revealed her sin. She has been playing with herself. She has been doing nasty things and she has molested other little girls, your daughters."

no longer talking
about my brothers
this changed tactic
a whole new
world of nasty
I had no voice
no defense
the old widow
reported back
to him, found
my *privates* were
red and irritated
suggested I might be
"playing" with myself
masturbating, not
even accidentally

gave him a hammer
new revolting
accusations
ripped into my ears

no sympathy
in the room full of eyes
daddy and mama
nowhere to be seen
molested their daughters?

Brother Leo
stabbed me with words
new and strange
watched me bleed
confusion
I wanted
to understand
but I had no library
for these expressions
"Molester of innocent little girls, lesbian, whore, deviant"

after dark
he sent me home
carrying a letter
for mama
she opened it
read it with tight lips
and furrowed brow
put me to bed
exhausted, confused
as a whipped pup
comforted only
when I curled up
into Esther's warmth
much as I could

she was sleeping
with a sheet
wrapped round her
knotted hard in the
middle of her back
Brother Leo's latest
torture device

for bed wetting
that, and dipping her
fingers in hot pepper oil
and turpentine
to keep her
from biting her nails

drifting sleepy
I heard mama again
fierce, angry
despairing, crying
pleading with daddy
grieving, giving up
heard the same words
"Molester of little girls, deviant, lesbian, whore, why? why?"
low-voiced reply
couldn't make
out everything

I'd heard before
in dogmatic sermons
"Whore of Babylon"
knew it was bad
could not place
myself into
the reference
I knew to be
defamations of
the Catholic church
and the pope

indescribably
exhausted, bruised
mind full of
roiling incoherent
thoughts and fearful
imaginings
I plummeted into
sleep, to harrowing

dreams of
snarling dogs
cracking
the bloody
bones of wicked
purple robed women

CHAPTER 27 – Assigned Chores

Age of accountability for kids

in The Park, was 12 years old
chores started much younger
Esther and I, now 7 years old

assigned to The Dining Hall
given instructions for
daily requirements

alarm rang right at 5:30
get up, get dressed
we did not snooze or linger

that lesson was quickly learned
assigned women would be
arriving to start cooking

always linked, holding hands
sometimes in the dark, we
walked down the sidewalk

to the Dining Hall, still
silent before breakfast
turned on the overhead lights

took down the metal chairs
folded and stacked atop
each of the eight tables, so

linoleum floors could be
mopped the night before
placed a row of chairs on

each side, carefully laid out
Corelle plates, the fork placed

to the left on a paper napkin

knife and spoon to the right
glasses placed in the space
just above the spoon

carefully, we carried
pitchers of water
and orange juice from

the refrigerators, placed
them in the middle
of the table, along

with cream and sugar
cups and saucers left by
the big pots for coffee

all year, every day
before school, before
our own breakfast

summer months, always
plenty of work, out by 6am
work until 2pm, washing, drying

piles of dishes, pulling weeds
raking lawns, sweeping patios
our evening chore, scrub

The Toddle House floor
on hands and knees
girls were given buckets

scrub brushes, old rags
we scrubbed in grids
each tile, a square foot

best way to get the tedious

chore done. Once a month
required to wax the floors

happily, we pulled each other
around on old towels
making joy in the way of

children free of watchers
buffed the whole thing to a
shine on our knees and butts

the boys in The Park cleaned
The Dining Hall floors
they were given mops

CHAPTER 28 – The Devil's Familiar

Excited word got around

in the long, hot summer
a big rattler was seen and

heard, winding round
up in the boulders

men planned a hunt
to flush him out

"We don't want any snake bites."

but…. I knew
it's really because

snakes are evil, like bats
and cats, all familiars

of witches and the devil
cannot be suffered to live

rampant faith, body sanctified
"They shall take up the serpent!"

believers will not be
harmed, yet no one believes

in grisly horned evil, the way
devout Godly people do

never left his rocky refuge
to hunt any of us, but

men and boys found him
with long sticks and shovels

hallooed, puffed up, brought
their prize back for viewing

silent unexpected pity
to see required death

fierce, fanged viper, forked
tongue limply extruded

delicate lacework scales
rippled down his back

mosaic diamond perfection
silvery gray, brown, and tan

symmetry interrupted
along his impressive length

with bloody wounds and
gaping evisceration

I had a strange notion
snakes do not bleed

stacked in a huge glass jar
coiled caricature of his

once springing vitality
lethal tension gone with his

crotalus oreganus animus
does he, in reverse, view

his own triangular head
venomous crucible, impotent?

dark lines running like paint
or tears, from eyes to jaws

black and white bands
just above bloodied rattle

warning system lifeless, on
lifeless convolutions

someone cut if off
with a skinning knife

kept it for a trophy
spectacular reptilian skin

made a fancy hat band

CHAPTER 29 – Projection and Opprobrium

Second grade without Esther

was frustrating
and so lonely
she and I had been
a flexible shadow
occupying
the same space

I adored school
enjoyed endless books
gradually drifted
away from
my responsible place
in front of her
preoccupied
with a new world
of line and phrase

barely finished
the first quarter
when I told a lie
one of those
falsehoods that fell
out of my mouth
before my brain
recognized
what I was saying

daily recess at school
interlude from
class, swinging
on the monkey bars
playing kick ball
time to relax, let
the breeze blitz cob webs

out of our brains
before returning to class
the school janitor
"Chuy" middle-aged
his wide brown
pock marked face
always seen on
the playground
he played tag
and teased us
tossing balls
back and forth
funny, in a not
completely
innocent way
goofing, grinning
at little girls
he'd run by and
flip their skirt up
mischievously, tag them

my sisters and other girls
our age at a Saturday
night sleep over
Sharon asked,
"Do you think Chuy is funny? He flipped my dress up."

my mouth opened
words came out
"He pulled up my dress and pulled down my panties."
no memory of thinking
them before
I said them
mama heard me
horrified, she
called for daddy
litany of questions
afraid now but
not sure how to fix it

I stuck to the lie
embellished it over
the next days
police were called
kids were removed
from the school
I remember a
strange night when
Chuy and his family
outsiders
knocked on
our door, wanted
to talk to me
daddy sent
them packing

one of the Brothers
had some notion of
the law and he
initiated a
legal action
against Chuy
and the school

I kept lying
even named six
grade schoolers
first names and last
who saw it happen
had no idea one
of the kids I named
was Chuy's grandson
added insult for
his family and mine
but I couldn't
seem to stop
I painted my self
tight into a corner
until I wished

I could just melt
disappear, become
part of the wall

the last official
to question me
a friendly policeman
Officer Boyd had been
to our classroom
and taught us a song
about safety
to look both ways
when crossing the street

he was large and seemed
invincible, with his
gun belt and flashlight
sitting on our couch
his eyes were direct
and kind, no fury
burned there
this policeman sang songs
with little kids
wanted them safe
he spoke softly, no
condemnation
simply asked

"Deborah, did you tell a lie?"

with flooding relief
I admitted the lie
a huge weight
lifted off my shoulders
hoped maybe
he *saw* through
his kind eyes
something amiss
but he left our house

I never saw him again
kids returned
to school and no one
ever questioned
why I would tell
a lie like that

the shame of it
stuck to me
identified as a liar
and a problem child
crushed, mama
had no internal
recognition
for why I would
lie this way, to her
it seemed to confirm
Brother Leo's words

she lost faith and
stopped trying
to shield me
the way folks looked
at me changed
a large sign
was created, a
sandwich board
dropped over
my head, to read
front and back

"I am a dirty liar!"
"I am as stubborn as a mule!"

trudged up and down
the roads of The Park
until dark, every day
after school
wearing that blasted

sign, suffered daily
abuses, extreme
attempt to cleanse me
moved back to
the home of
Brother Leo's
brother- in- law
slept on the floor
in their baby's room

every morning
before school
a different Brother
showed up to
administer a beating
I never knew what
was coming, a belt, a switch
once an electric cord
excruciating pain, worse
than anything so far
I walked to school
every day, red striped
throbbing pain, layered
over black and blue
from neck to knees

though dressed
neck to knees
a matter of modesty
I am sure belt welts
and bruises
could be seen
but I was the little girl
told a nasty lie
about the nice janitor
idiot author
of my own troubles
I began to hate myself
began to wonder

why I was born
they think I deserve it, maybe I do....

I started to feel
even own
I was bad seed
if they could
get rid of me
they would

I was an annoyance
foisted on a
young mother
accidentally
shut her baby's
finger in the
sliding door of
the bedroom
to keep him
from crawling
out of the room
she said, I did
it on purpose
accused of fresh lies
no sanctuary
whether I lied or not

life became a series
of interrogations
I could not withstand
I found myself
in the brown bathroom
over and over again
my anxiety and fear grew
I was no longer surprised
by any new evil
The Servant of The Lord
saw in me

weeks later, I was sent
back home again
it felt alien
accept to crawl
into our bed and
lay my head on
the pillow I
shared with Esther
she automatically
curled into me
offered what she could

CHAPTER 30 – Monopoly and Rebellion

We could never win that dratted game

but how we
loved to play Monopoly
creased, raggedy old game
mama bought
at the Bargain Basement
set it up on the table
divvy the money
happy dickering
swapping of
properties, tossing
around hundreds
of dollars
high rollers in a
spartan single wide
obedient life metered
in a religious swamp
for our games
minimal rules
Johnny and Tony
cheated, no shame

watch out for Sharon
she'd win while
the rest of us
traded like maniacs
borrowed money
like madmen, always
some kerfuffle over
pewter board pieces
least desirable, thimble
iron, hat, or shoe.
squabbled over cannon, car,
horse, dog, and ship.
drew straws to decide

Johnny and Tony
cheated at that too

Tony made popcorn
in a beat-up pan
thin layer of hot oil
kernels added, waited
pop…pop……. pop, pop, pop
clap on the lid
shake, shake, shake
across the burner,
like a flurried chef
always buttery
salty, rarely burned

evening, daddy and mama
out at a tape lesson
five kids absorbed
in a noisy game
a knock on the door
Brother Joe, with a
summons for
Johnny and Tony
"For a lesson"

did he feel bad about stealing away children from a parentless house?
did any of them ever recognize the fear and dread, the black shroud
they brought with their summons?

always trouble,
when a summons came
fun misted away like vapor
expectant fear in its place
sadly, we were like
those popcorn kernels
pinioned in cold
congealed butter
helpless to flee

*another lesson, how many could they endure? they always came home
demoralized, Tony withdrawn, Johnny with another hotly forged layer of armor*

Johnny, head up
asked defiantly
"Should I bring my bible to the lesson?"
sniggering reply
"No, you won't be needing it."

told me they
whispered about
running away
as they walked
to their lesson
decided they
had nowhere to go
no money to go
on their own

Johnny assured Tony
"Don't worry, I'll make Ole Leo so mad he'll be worn out by the time he gets to you"
and he tried
as was his way
but he couldn't
save Tony
got for himself
double portion
of bloody agony

left on our own,
scared, anxious, we packed
up our old game
we were sleeping
when one of our older
brothers woke us up,
said we needed a lesson
immediate coiling fear,
snapping dread

trouble!

rumpled sleepy
Sharon, Esther, and I
huddled close
prodded to move
reluctantly
down the hall
into the living room

trouble!

miasma
wormed in the air
thick, hot, coppery

blood?

Johnny, on his knees,
in front of the couch
naked except
for his underwear
I'd never seen him
in his underwear
I'd never seen him cry
only ever seen his bravado
and irreverence
ripping embarrassment
terrible gutting grief for him

trouble!

had they managed it this time, did they finally break him?

forearms on the couch
head hanging
whole body quivering with
muted distress, gritted teeth

struggling to contain howls
of outrage and pain
my mind could not
make sense of the
bloody lashings on his back

I can never unsee
his white underwear
stuck to his butt
in jagged red stripes
of fresh blood

it's blood! they have whipped him bloody! where's Tony
where is daddy? where is mama? are we next?

fully awake now
eyes wide, brain cranking
reeling, frame by frame
blink, blink, flash
visualized trauma
encapsulated in
technicolor
waking nightmares
for my future

hot tears falling
noses running, we
cried quietly, carefully
Esther, behind me
threw up, no gagging
just a cascade of hot
vomit down my back
rising sour smell added
to the pall of wretched fear

we didn't see the beating but we saw the results, in this case, our older brother did not inflict the beating, he just delivered the message to the rest of us, but the lesson we learned we were not safe from older siblings. The serpent's social experiment, diminish the elderly parents, raise up the younger, give them power over the youngest

sternly instructed to
get cleaned up, get to bed
as if we were not filled with
quivering fear, had not
just witnessed
unparalleled abuse
degradation

where was the almighty, to stay the hand of the abusers?

daddy and mama
released from their lesson
after the fact
too much, *"Phileo love,"*
daddy impotent
mama weakened, weary
weeping once again
while she
washed the blood out
of their bed sheets

Johnny fought with them
threw a few punches
paid in blood
but he got harder
hell-bent on his own path
dry eyed, stony surrenders
he bowed to the lash
externally tough, but
creeping internal insecurity
became teenage
nocturnal enuresis
for this, he was put outside, up
amongst trees and boulders
behind the house
denounced

"Go sleep like an animal."

pounding rain
crashing thunder
dark, dark night
allowed to run up
there to get him out
of the deluge, soaking wet
holding flashlights
illuminated Johnny

sound asleep
under a huge
piece of plastic
rain dripping
running in rivulets
off the drape
joined streaming
runnels
winding away
to lower ground

*Johnny and Tony still carry the scars of that beating. I confirmed this story with them
I have always been confident of my memories, but I'm still running from the shade, cast by
a liar*

CHAPTER 31 – Mama is Thrown Out

Mama could take no more, temper raging, went after Brother Leo

a useless battle
accused of
inappropriate
"Phileo love"
banished from
The Park
daddy let it happen
taking faith
in the words
of The Prophet
"Go on ahead Brother Daulton, I see it all coming out OK."

bought her a
bus ticket
she walked
Brother Leo's
gauntlet to the
entrance of
The Park
reminiscent of
the Prophet's
last visit
vastly different

she went back
home to Kentucky
was gone for
many weeks
we stayed with
designated
Park dwellers
mama sent
letters and a few
hard earned packages

came in the mail
long flannel
nightgowns with
a rooster on the front
and a ruffle around
the bottom
and knee socks
two pairs for
all three of us

not pastel
pink or blue
like the other girls
dark mustard yellow
but worn with
enthusiasm
all the same
long enough
to pull up
to our knees
and fold
over, once

mama lasted
several weeks
away from her kids
before deciding
to come back
hold her peace
bend to a force
she couldn't fight

when she
returned home
directives were
established
she would
take medicine
for her nerves

CHAPTER 32 – The Big Patio

The cement truck rolled slowly

through
the entrance
of The Park
it seemed too big
for the narrow dirt roads
children, tuned
to a winding zephyr
heads lifted
senses amplified
to an escaped
lamp genie
strangeness
from habitual
Park events
compelled to run
go and see!

immediate
delight in a
new experience
lumbering old rig
huge round tumbler
bed, turning
we knew where
it was going
we followed
like a noisy
gaggle of
adolescent ducks

watched it
slowly creep
heard reverberant
beep.... beep.... beep
as it backed
into place
and like a dusty
dung beetle
slowly extruded
a long nozzle
with a viscid *glug*
cement began
pouring into
the preformed
border of
The Big Patio

the Brothers
dug out
footings and built
the border
now, they stood
with long
wooden poles
each had an
attachment
to pull across
the surface
for smoothing

uncanny how
lumpy gray sludge
became a
landmark for
my young life
it took days
to dry
the minute
we were allowed

we raced
out onto the
flat rectangular
grey surface

most of the
outdoor events
happened on
The Big Patio
the Brothers built
half-walls
and a large roof
like an open air
amphitheater
picnic tables
for summer
outdoor eating
nighttime
reel to reel
movies, *The Bible*
The Story of Ruth
Joan of Arc, The Robe

when chores
were done and
nothing was
scheduled
we were given
permission to
skate there
one of the Brothers
procured a big box of
old roller skates
metal ones
came in pieces
hooked onto the
bottom of our shoes
he helped us

sort them out
oiled them
polished away
the rusty spots
even found
a few keys
joyous weeks
we spent
exchanging parts
borrowing keys
to tighten
loosen, re-fit

daringly
we rumbled
down one of the
long steep
flagstone sidewalks
flying, thumpity......bump
luminescent
limbic pleasure
wind in my hair
a certain
hapless freedom

we dickered
and traded for
pieces and parts
old keys
leather straps
and buckles
packets of Kool-Aid
Bazooka bubble gum
with a cartoon folded
in the wrapper
broken toys
and a raggedy kite
missing a tail

seemed like
we had fifty siblings
forged strong bonds
many exist today

Summer, two o'clock afternoon snack

kids grouped at The Big Patio
for half a popsicle, maybe ice cream
or homemade oatmeal cookies
sometimes a carefully coordinated

sneak attack, to administer
a dose of nutrition all kids hate
liver and fish, combined in a huge
greasy spoonful of cod liver oil

cold and nasty, slimy, like glue
it stuck to my tongue, coated
my mouth, fishy taste eased
only to be burped right back

little kids, noses pinched
spooned in, soon as open mouth
facilitated breathing
older kids understood, swallow

gagging, spitting out, or throwing
up, meant a second spoonful
orders had been given, no
inclination to disobedience

for the Sisters, snack time was story
time, they read to us, carefully chosen
passages from the Bible, or bits
from *"The Life Story"* of the Prophet

read about him working as a cowboy
here in Arizona, a ranger in Indiana
a Golden Gloves boxer, a lineman
and a young preacher, whom God

spoke to, revealed his truth for
the coming apocalyptic rapture

gave him the commandments for
believers of the end time *"The Message"*

no way we could have known, he was
never a Golden Gloves Boxer, actually
a bill collector for the power company
and his revealed truths, plagiarized

but the story they read, that filled
my mind, sunk into my soul, kept me
wakeful, worried, and fearful
a small book, *"Raptured"*

written in 1950 by Rev Ernest Angley
a story of two good people
Hester Bell Wilson and Jim Collins
both good kids, raised in church

taught all of their lives
about the coming rapture
both reminded daily to be ready
both, *left behind!*

Hester, taken by the regime, clung to her Christian teachings

"Her eyes sparkled like diamonds, and there was a halo of glory around her head. In a sweet voice she cried, 'No, a thousand times no! Soon I'll be with him who died for me!' She stood chained to the stake, her Bible held to her heart, lips moving in prayer while she was surrounded by the red searing flames."

Jim chose the opposite path, joined the regime, took the Mark of the Beast

"Jim stood watching Mary die. He detested the sight of her and he was glad she was being put to death. Her head rolled down into the gutter. Jim picked it up by the hair, and like a maniac he slung it round and round, spraying blood, shouting glory and honor to the Beast. The earth began to shake with mighty force. The stars fell onto the earth. Jim fell at the foot of the huge rocks and mountains, 'Rocks be merciful, fall on me, fall on me!'"

emphatic doctrine, glorious
Christianity in the face of death
eaten by lions, beheaded, torn
asunder, burned at the stake

reprobate mind, insanity
suicidality, for the
unrepentant, gory descriptions
for a no-win scenario

for young children an effective sell
our only sin, impressionability
we soaked up propagandized fear,
imprinted deeply for any, *left behind!*

insidiously, young minds
were tuned like radios
to one frequency

"Trust and obey, for there's no other way, to be happy in Jesus, but to trust and obey."

The Big Patio and its central location

became the place to direct
folks for any orders given
kids gathered for daily
work assignments

marching lessons, drills
started there, formed up
shortest to tallest, boys
in one group, girls in the other

left…right…left…right…left…right
stayed at it until perfect formation
"About face…knees high……forwaaaard march…. company halt…....at ease!"

we found this joyful
and fun, something we
enjoyed as a group
stomping down the roads

singing, encouraged to shout
at the top of our lungs
ringing endorsement for
pervasive brainwashing

"I'm in the Lord's army! I'm in the Lords army! I'm too young to march in the infantry, shoot the artillery, I'm too young to zoom o're the enemy, but I'm in the Lord's army!"

conditioned to enjoy
exuberantly believe and
willingly comply with
expected, aligned behavior

Like the town square or pillory

The Big Patio was a place to
witness designated discipline
and stern reprisals for
infractions or disobedience
harder though, to fit the
scope of Godly correction
to actual experience

brain rattling confusion in witnessed
humiliations, stupefying perversions
of our fundamental indoctrination
chastised boys, helpless to
prevent the removal of elemental
religious security, maleness

heads shaved, lined up like a cabaret troupe
dressed like girls, wearing frilly skirts
ear bobs, lip stick, garish eye shadow
black tar mascara on tear-streaked faces
belt welts visible on skinny boy legs
lacy panties cupped prized male genitals

exposed by lifted skirts, photos snapped
adults encouraged to point and ridicule
testament to our own
*"Lucifer effect, good
people can be induced, seduced and
initiated into behaving in evil ways."*
unresearched, unheard of
in the sixties, abhorrently active
in our pious God-fearing community

for kids, nothing to do but
survive, keep breathing, eat, sleep
wait, with helpless resignation, for
whatever increasingly creative
punishment would come next

CHAPTER 33 – Root Cellars

Used for food storage and horrid discipline

the root cellars
two of them
small caverns
dug into dirt banks
near the creek
at the outer southern
edge of The Park
fortified wooden
shelves, laden
with mason jars
of canned food
earthily fecund
dank and cool
hellishly black
when the door
closed, bolted
from the outside

single metal chair
placed at the center
between upright
log supports
home to spiders
centipedes, stink bugs
occasional snakes
and large rats
a perfect choice
for terrifying
confinement
creepy in daylight
ghoulish heart clanging
misery at night
deemed a valuable lesson
consequence

for disobedience
perceived infractions

accustomed
to fear, resistance
beaten out of us
each new penance
eclipsed the last
a single day
in the root cellar
held a forever taint
and creeping horror
for me, catatonic fear
and numbness
surrounded me
like a fuzzy aura
reality faded, nothing
but the sound
of huffing breath

naked tailed rats
rustling along the
walls, couldn't tell
where they were
till they got close
enough to explore
frightened, kicking
scrabbling feet, but
more afraid of
stealthy spiders
living arachnophobia
cringing panic
breathless nausea
all of this, we suffered
alone in the dark

could be for almost
anything, we knew reasons
were crafted fancies

of the puppeteer
jerking the strings
on his deaf and dumb
adult minions

I wonder if he enjoyed watching them obey
give up their most precious gifts, without question?

Tony, condemned
to three days and
God-awful nights
in the root cellar
given only
bread and water
and a coffee can
to pee in
left in that
stinking blackness
like a prisoner of war
door bolted behind him

we all knew
the horror of the
damp dirty place
skin shuddering
imagination
made it even worse
centipedes, spiders
crawling on him
under his clothes
he would have no way
to see them coming
no defense

Johnny, always
our valiant hero
left the house
late at night
armed with a

flashlight and food
endured the black hole
alongside him
and snuck away
early, before
rising adults

Johnny, Tony, Sharon, Esther, and I, knew nothing of PTSD, we lived with our nightmares, reactivity and quirks, conditions created in budding minds. Physically we survived the hot bed of blind obedience, dictated abuses, horrible shit not contemplated by the average mind. We existed, without choice, in bondage to a zealously preached overlay.

All of our suffering was making us good enough to go to heaven, live a beautiful life, in a beautiful land, beyond the sky, where we would sit at the feet of Jesus, and worship in golden splendor forever, and ever, Amen.

CHAPTER 34 – Sister Joan's Exorcism

After our chores and 2 o'clock snacks we had free hours

until dark
every age child
played together
formed bands
stormed forts
carried away captives
ransomed
with Kool-Aid
made in an old
bleach bottle
eagerly anticipated
treat, undrinkable

we came down
from the rocks
snuck to The Dining Hall
where the best
rhubarb grew
stolen, it seemed
better, tangy sweet
the broad leaves
made great roofs
for our forts

Sister Joan
startled us when
she stepped
out the back door
inexplicably odd
with crooked teeth
and puffy gums
mouth always
gluey, she needed
to consider words

her speech slow
thickly garbled
this day she seemed
distant, distracted
tuned inward
to her aura
silent herald
for an arriving
paroxysm, she
stared sightless
and then dropped
like a bomb
into the ripe
rhubarb plants

her head jerked back
arms and legs
twitched, an
involuntary gambol
guttural sounds
scraped from
her throat
neck veins popped out
face congested red
followed by
alarming blue
jaw clenched
bloody strings
of saliva wound
across her face
into her ears

one of us, present
enough to run
screaming for help
the rest of us
horridly fascinated
watched her
writhing seizure

smash the rhubarb flat
her modest dress
rucked up
pale limbs flailed
sharp scent of
urine rose
from crushed
rhubarb plants
I could see she
had no control
over this vicious thing
unraveling her body

several Sisters
arrived with some
of the Brothers
one hollered
about possession
Legion, the devil
and evil spirits
raced to the water spigot
and hosed her down
I'd never seen
an epileptic fit, we
watched wide eyed
the depravity
that followed
callous, casting out
of the devil

adults formed
a semi-circle, began to
pray, no attempt
was made to
protect her, no
comfort offered
simply pious intent
drive out demons
with cold water

and ignorance

she choked
aspirated and
thrashed, until
it was over
she, helpless
as one of us
couldn't have
been long, though
it seemed like forever
until she went still
sprawled limp

underlying
jubilant praise and
thanks to the Lord
insensate, sonorous
respirations
she didn't come
around quickly
remained immobile
in the wet
muddy rhubarb
finally, two Brothers
hoisted her up
beneath her arms
and knees, set her
in a large wheelbarrow

took her home
head rolled sideways
dilute blood trickled
from her lips and chin
wet legs dangled
over the end
soaked hair and clothes
left a trail of dribbles
on the sunny sidewalk

we watched them
vanish in the arid heat
insubstantial vapor
as if they were never there

we broke from the
outlandish exorcism
scattered back
to the rocks
and trees of
our summer forts
new empathy
for a simple adult
caught in the same
trap with us
rhubarb
forever altered
in my memory

CHAPTER 35 – Elk's Theater

Daddy's enduring love for western movies

created a wonderful memory I have of
him joining us in surreptitious activity

Butch Cassidy and The Sundance Kid
came to the Elk's Theater, September 1969
daddy couldn't help himself, he wanted

to see that movie, the best way to do that
take all of us to the movie with him
he piled us in the car, heads kept lowered

below the windows, quietly drove out
of The Park the back way, bouncing over
over rocks, splashing through the creek

In 1905, Elks Lodge #330, built the
wonderfully Victorian opera house and
theater, a regal copper Elk proudly

poised on the top of the building
old fashioned recessed area facing the
street, held the lighted box office and

a walking area on either side to buy soda pop
chocolate covered raisins, and long-lasting suckers
before finding seats in the opulent red chairs

expectantly waited for the dramatic red drape
to open on the movie, we enjoyed watching
Butch Cassidy and the Sundance Kid

every single night for a solid week
my memory of daddy's joy, the feeling
of sharing this illicit excitement with him

by far, the greater pleasure
it did not last long

CHAPTER 36 – Runaway

We wakened from a nap on a quiet afternoon

to rhythmic swats outside the
window, a sound we recognize

immediately, the slapping of a
leather belt, in brutal symphony

with strangled spitting cries
instant fear, welling gut reaction

my eyes connected with Esther's
quietly, in unison, we slid from bed

slunk low, to hide beneath the window
memory from daddy's war stories

how he scootched under a window sill
laid in the shadow beneath to evade

enemy soldiers peering through
slowly, I raised up to peek over the sill

scared, frantic, Esther pulled at me
collar choked hard against my throat

Johnny, under the lash again
sitting on a chair, bare feet on

an upturned bucket, face red
defiant with stubborn endurance

lashes blazed across his naked feet
he must have run away……again

slid back down to sit, hands tightly clasped

white knuckled, we listened to his torment

and interrogation, got caught in the act
this time, ran off into the boulders

up through the trees behind our trailer
winding dirt trail to the Rodeo Grounds

home of *"The World's Oldest Rodeo"*
and Prescott Downs, part time race track

Johnny found smelly solace, soul connection
with horses, he could hardly hide where he'd

been, he reeked of grassy manure
and oiled leather, he mucked stinky stalls

groomed and worked horses, soothed his soul
with soft whickers, his natural cowboy spirit

melded with equine totem, stabilized fiery
internal conflict with flying centaur freedom

always on the wrong end of a thrashing
we could tell beating him didn't work

just made him harder, angrier, more
determined, he snuck out anyway, same

painful night, feet battered with hot
red belt welts, pulled on his boots, hobbled

off in the dark, over the rocky trail
clinging to iron will, inch by painful

inch, like a doomed crab, trying
to creep out of the bucket

Eventually this became somewhat positive for Johnny

when one of the Brothers
started a business using

a couple of mules and *"Pal"*
a big yellow draft horse

to haul huge logs down the
wooded ridges way out

in the back country, Johnny
handled them naturally

one afternoon, mama was
standing at the stove when he

opened the door, slid silently
into the trailer, furtive glance

side to side, hypervigilant
distressed, ready for trouble

eyes blinking from a dark
gruesome blood mask

dried, cracking, with
fresh blood running

in front of his ears
and dripping off

his chin, white tee shirt
saturated, stuck to

his chest and stomach
mama stared, *"Oh My Lord Jesus!"*

grabbed a dishtowel

pressed it on the

gaping laceration at
the top of his head

"Lord have mercy! What happened?"

an argument with one
of the older teens

working with other boys
Johnny would not have

tolerated any guff from
a kid near his own age

would have been in fight mode
instantly, the older teen

whacked him in the
head with a 2x4

drove off in the truck
left him to walk home

several miles on foot
bleeding from a deep head

wound, the case against
him already made

daddy arrived home, primed
with the first boy's story

pushed mama down
in a kitchen chair, left

her sitting, bloody
dish towel in her hands

hauled Johnny, still bleeding
from the gash in his scalp

to The Garage at the
far north side of The Park

The Servant of the Lord
daddy, and the Brothers

set those boys to fight
like chained yard dogs

Johnny gave up reason
and became a rabid beast

didn't care about injury, long
as he could inflict damage

driven, raging fury of fists
feet, elbows, and knees

unleashed, rampant payback
for his torment delivered

Christianity aside
the Brothers, heated

with blood lust, wanted
more, a second fight

matched Johnny with
another boy, unrelated

to the event, this one
just for fun, but a

handicap was needed
our oldest brother

smacked him across
both shins with a metal bar

hoary men goaded the bulls
pricked them to savagery

intense male response to blood
and sweat, still not enough

they may have noted possible
permanent, even fatal injury

for Johnny, so far undefeated
continuing to berserker brawl

decided to match other
teen boys like prized cocks

caged, ruffled, helpless against
the lust for more combat

pulled Tony into their ring
made him fight too, a friend

the younger brother of the kid
bashed Johnny in the head

CHAPTER 37 – Freedom Train

I made it to 4th grade, 1970

the five of us
adjusted to new
and different abuses
existed in a
shame based life
summons were normal
but we survived
Johnny ran off
to the horse track
Tony found refuge
in withdrawal, creating
building, crafting
Sharon and I, in books
Esther, chewed her
fingernails to bloody nubs
undeterred by pepper oil
and turpentine

finally, upstairs at
school, many new books
Harriet Tubman
"Freedom Train"
felt her bondage in my soul
this female Moses
"Charlie and the Chocolate Factory"
a poor boy
got the golden ticket
other worldly
"A Wrinkle in Time"
kids who could
fold existence
"Rikki Tikki Tavi"
epic battle, little mongoose
wicked hooded cobra

adored biographical
books, and Native
American History
found a set of ugly old
orange bound books
delved into the life stories
of *Abe Lincoln, Madame Curie*
Mary Todd Lincoln, George Washington
Tecumseh, General Robert E Lee, Ulysses Grant
Andrew Jackson, Geronimo, Crazy Horse
Black Elk, Sitting Bull, Sequoia, Osceola
Squanto, Sacagawea, Cynthia Ann Parker
and her son, *Quanah Parker*
I imagined running away
to be adopted
by the Indians

I lived for sneaky moments
gave every book
the benefit of
total immersion
waited for the
expected moment
when reality faded to black
and I lost myself
in the story
identified with
dynamic protagonists
imagined myself
in feathers and beads
or completely protected
in golden armor

ending a book
agitated me, returned
searching, restless spirit
I needed to
blink, blink, blink
re-orient to the present

rein in my brain
restart mundane
until my addiction
required a fix
then, I found
frantic purpose
in the solid weight
of tome and page
calm restored
mind centered
quiet again
open for
another escape

CHAPTER 38 - Rabbit Stew

I watched, afraid to object

understanding well
a new game of death
and the making
of fresh nightmares

they came for
our pet rabbits
pink eyed Rosie
her snow-white fur
speckled with bits
of green food pellets
and straw bedding
wriggling frantically
she *screamed!*
internal reaction
to impending death
ululant human sounds
I didn't know a
pet rabbit could make

held, dangling by
her hind legs, bashed
on the back of her
head with a
heavy iron bar
thrashing suddenly stilled
her offspring
now equally riled
but neatly trapped
in the wooden hutch
suffered the same fate

no longer really
shocked by any event
I witnessed, still
I couldn't keep
hot tears from
tumbling down
my face, just
another cruel lesson
required by
The Servant of The Lord

children must be
aware of the
required supplies
to feed them every day
what edible animals
could be killed for
lifesaving meals
during the end of days
and tribulation
when we can
neither buy
nor sell

I felt profound shame
in the tiny flickering
sense of relief, it
was Rosie and her babies
not me
fluffy white, tan
black, brown,
spotted, silky soft
pet rabbits
dead, limp
heaped into
wheelbarrows
like offal

grisly sacrifice

to food stores
heart wrenching
painful, we only thought
we were somewhat inured
to death of our pets

beheaded, pelts
ripped off, tiny carcasses
cracked, split, and quartered
put into big stew pots
with new potatoes
onions, carrots, and peas
reluctant but pitifully
obedient kids
required to eat
that stew for dinner
at The Toddle House
served by women
mothers, aunties
sisters, grandmothers

how did this make them feel?
did they see this as a valid learning curve?
was this a normal action for necessary food?
maybe it was the times we lived in
not too far from memories of WWII
many of them must have seen this as a very matter of fact lesson

still, it wounded
my heart, I felt
physical cramping pain
it didn't kill me
I told myself
over and over
I didn't really eat
Rosie or her babies
they were likely
in the stew
one of the other kids ate

CHAPTER 39 – Efficient Beatings

Whipping sessions became the norm

so many kids
to beat in a day
the Brothers
began to recognize
fatigued necks
arms, shoulders
they needed
a remedy

did they have a think tank?
did they brainstorm?
did they ask the Lord to speak to them?
how do we beat a lot of children efficiently?

consensus reached
they'd use two men
to hold each child firm
but they found
tender skin often
bounces away
from the impact
of a leather belt
wielded by
such large men

little hands and arms get in the way
none of us could contain the need to reach back
cover our butts, squirm, wriggle, and twist
flexible, slippery, like landed trout

impossible to
hold us still and
beat us at
the same time

They devised a simple but efficient
way to keep us in place and get the
required punishment accomplished

they turned one

of those awful
metal folding chairs
around, pushed it
against the wall
placed us
behind the chair
and forced us
to bend over the back
reach down
place our hands
on the seat
or grip the side bars
if we were tall enough
if not, hands
were placed on
the back of the chair

> *thus, we anchored ourselves for our beatings*
> *the back of the chair against the chest of*
> *the smaller children, wedged into the gut of the*
> *larger kids, we could not bounce away*
> *we quickly learned if we let go of that chair*
> *the misery would start all over again*

standing on
either side
of a helpless
positioned child
two men went to work
alternating lashes
beatings went
faster, Godly correction
was not so difficult

> *we children watched*
> *felt.... this evolution*
> *in technique*
> *unwittingly aided them*
> *in pursuing lengthier sessions*

CHAPTER 40 – The Worst Beating

Brother Leo's trailer sat

right on the
creek bank
a desirable
secluded spot
looking out
toward the
rippling water
elegant
flagstone
steps curved
down the bank

he didn't like
weeds and brush
blocking his
sparkling view
the kids, conscripted
weeded the banks
of the creek
all the way
though The Park
lined each bank
with smooth
stones pulled
from the water
running along
each side
neat as a
cobbled wall

started at daylight
we worked very hard
in the summer
school is out
the punishments

are worse
age did not matter
we found joy in
each other, began
funny chain stories
taking turns
to enliven and
create bigger
fantastical additions
someone added
a talking elephant
on a journey
to fix his voice
cause no one
could understand
a word he said
searching, he found
a wise man
learned the secret, he
must lift his trunk high
before speaking
to un-garble
his enunciations

innocent fun
delighted giggling
almost lunch time
when Brother Will appeared
at the top of the
creek bank
everything changed
and turned bleak
like a sudden
thunderstorm

in his hand
a lined piece
of paper
a dreaded list

children stilled
suddenly silent
like flitting happy birds
we reacted to the predator
in our trilling woods
tense, waiting
hoping to sink
and disappear into
the weeds and rocks
slide into the burbling creek
gently float away

directed to
The Toddle House
where we normally
ate lunch
frightfully quiet
we filed in, no gaggle
of noisy children
all lost in churning
knowledge and fear
tables not set
no food, no water
for hot children
working all morning
in the Arizona sun

there is only the list
and our chastisers
Brother Will and Brother Tim
deputed to mete out
the punishment

on the list
next to each name
a number
how many lashes
each child would get
numbers uncommonly

large that day
50, 75, 100, 125, 150

There, next to my name, 150

one hundred and fifty!
panic, so ripe
my throat closes
I can't swallow
never had that many
25 or 30 lashes
leave welts
and bruises
last for weeks

shared misery
envelopes the room
like tender green vines
we curl inward
empathetically
winding together
all we can do
is watch
and count

"One…two…three….four."
thwack…thwack…. thwack…. thwack!

the counting
becomes inexorable
as the beatings
robotic reaction
nervous dread
possible attempt
to be certain
none of us
would get
one more lash
than is
ordered
"Fourteen…fifteen…sixteen"
thwack…thwack…thwack!

some kids, older
keep it together
bent over, clutching
both sides of the seat
writhing with
each strike
faces in rictus
teeth clenched
tears, snot
running
mingling
strangled bleats
escaping
the two men
on either side
continue to
alternate lashes

thwack…thwack…thwack!

on and on and on

"Forty-one…forty-two…forty-three"

Danny Bill, face
bone white under
spattered freckles
lurches away
frantic attempt
to dodge
breathing hard
Brother Tim
grabs Danny Bill
twists large fists
into the front
of his shirt
picks him up high

his feet dangle

helplessly
a shoe drops
to the floor
Brother Tim
smashes him
backward
his small round
head goes
right through
the drywall

pausing, still
huffing through
his nose
Brother Tim says,
"Anyone else want to run?"
dead silence
disbelief
head shaped
hole in the wall
subdued now
Danny Bill
takes his beating
and on it goes
each in turn
counting down
every strike
of the belt

"Fifty…fifty-one…fifty-two"
thwack…thwack…thwack!

I hear my name
clammy, frantic
fear, fizzing
disassociation
it's not me
moving
walking to

the flogging chair

terror racks my body
an endless shudder
speeds up my heart
steals my breath
morphs to
unseen creature
clawing me from inside
the urge to pee
is horribly strong
intestines rumble

instinctively
I tuck a
primordial tail
hard and tight
the creeping
distortion
slinks downward
my knees feel
boneless, I look
down at them
expecting eels
where my lower
legs should be
nothing but summer
dress and tennis shoes
raging fight or flight
can't fight
nowhere to run

I can feel
the loss of control
coming on
I can't.... *think*
through the
muddle in
my mind

can't check it as
the counting starts
for me

"One!"

first *thwack!*
hurts like blazes
across my butt
a streaking, cutting
razor of fire

moving, jumping
I hit the wall
hoping for a hole
a time warp to
anywhere but here
Brother Will
grabs my arm
hauls me back
grinning widely

"Whoooeeee, I didn't think she could move that fast!
right over the back of the chair, just like a monkey!"

he turns to
Brother Tim
chortling
slapping his knee
handsome
looming monster
entertained
in a room full
of inconsolable
children

Brother Tim
joins him, chuckling
wipes his sweaty brow
with a forearm
my face fills with hot
blood, a surging feeling
embarrassment
so intense
it outweighs
the impact
of the beating
hot shame explodes
into determination
they will *never*
laugh at
me again

second time today
I bend over the chair
not quite tall enough
to place my palms
on the seat, grab the sides
the count starts over

"One…two…three"
thwack…thwack…thwack!
God, it hurts!

hell, on fire
nerve endings flash
hunching inward
each *thwack*
elicits a screech
but I do not move
helped by the chair
wedged into
my chest and stomach
the horrid metal thing
is now my support

"Twenty…twenty-one…twenty-two"

thwack…thwack…thwack!

shoulders, back
butt, and thighs
all the way down
to my knees
hot myriad of
flashing
searing pain

surreal tolerance
develops
becomes part
of the horrific
every lash
one more flame
it can't get worse

but then it does
a wild swing, the
loosened end of
the belt
curls under
my arm
around my ribs
slashes untouched
flesh, that new scald
intensely multiplied

I would find the
large red belt welt
ripped right across
immature breast
and nipple
fiery red
shaped like
the end of the belt

my clothes
rubbed and burned
that spot for days

"Ninety…. ninety-one…. ninety-two"
thwack…. thwack……thwack!

childhood companions
counting for me
eventually
"One hundred and fifty"
carried on
quavering voices
fellow victims
some still waiting
their turn

it is finally over
my entire body quivers
peripheral vision is cloudy
getting back to my seat
the focal pinpoint
my face and lips are numb
tingling, I am not sure if
I am breathing
wobbling knees
somehow support me
as I carefully sit
nerve endings seared
back, butt, and legs
beaten and bruised like
never before

egregious day
ended with prayer
Brother Will and Brother Tim
finished chastising
have us on our knees
the linoleum floor

hard, but somehow
softer than
our whip masters
they entreat God to
save our souls, to
recognize the benefit
of holy correction
never recognizing
the peril in which
their own
are swamped

kneeling obediently
I can't think
I can't pray
my body feels
like tenderized meat
a massive thumping
web of volcanic fire
I want mama
she'll put me
in a warm bath
soothe
my injuries
while she
weeps

I will be unbearably
sore and stiff
for the next
several days, sleeping
on my stomach to
endure the nights
after that
we resilient kids
will be in our forts
comparing belt welts
extreme stripes
dark blood pooled

near the
surface of
our skin
it's what we do

CHAPTER 41 – Serpent's Seed

Jesus said, "Suffer the children to come unto me."

but I don't think he
meant me, a child
yet somehow different
"Serpent's seed, born with lies on your tongue. Stubborn as a mule."
likely he didn't have
a place for me

Brother Leo
pontificated from
his brown toilet
Biblical references
from the garden
Eve *"knew"* the serpent
and she *"knew"* Adam
thus, she bore twins
one good, Abel
son of Adam
and one evil, Cain
"Serpent's Seed"

he described
wicked women
filthy sluts, whores
descendants of Eve
lower in creation
than dogs or hogs
he painted graphic
images of murder
perpetrated by
one evil brother
on his good brother
he named me *"Serpent's Seed"*
akin to the ill-bred Cain
bashed his brother's

brains out

"*Another Esau*"
he had to get me
away from Esther
before I could
bring about her ruin
steal the birthright
belonged rightfully
the second twin
according to
the word of God

I knew, a child who
is barely tolerated
does not deserve love
I stopped asking questions
fear overcame
innate curiosity
lost and uncertain
childish faith stomped
and fragmented
I continued to lie
everything got twisted
in my head
what came out
of my mouth
was never what
I intended
I could not fathom
this uncontainable
thing in my skull
consequence
would happen either way

poor mama worried
struggled, wept
tried to believe
I was not a born liar

she, my tiny refuge
until the black day, I pushed
her too far, told one lie too many

told her I apologized
to Sister Mary
for using a
black marker
to trace over
the name
Sharon Rose
in cursive script
soft and elegant
so beautifully
written on
a pale manilla
school folder
from The Chapel
now, obscured
ruined by heavy black
letters globbed
together, a
messy smudge
Sharon Rose
only faintly
visible underneath

I did go
to the chapel
stared at the door
sat on the stone wall
out front
kicked loose rocks
fiddled with
sticky pine cones
braided pine needles
gone from

green to brown

I just couldn't do it
couldn't knock
on that door
face what I knew
would follow
convinced myself
mama would never know
but she went to ask
Sister Mary
if I apologized
she returned from
The Chapel
bitterly furious
disbelieving
"I don't know what to do with you? Why did you lie? I gave you a chance to tell the truth! Are they right? Is there something wrong with you? Are you a liar?"

I stared at her
dumb, stolid as an ox
mama responded
her conflicted frustration
and anger ruled
she cut a long switch
from the willow
in the yard
whipped me good
before she grabbed
me by my hair and
yanked me down
the sidewalk
to the road
I stumbled along
hands flailing
reaching, trying
to ease the
pain in my scalp
I fell hard and

never got back
on my feet

my shoes flew off
dirt and rocks
abraded my knees
skinned my toes
as mama dragged
me through the gravel
thumped me over
the raised sill
at The Dining Hall
dropped me
on the floor, like
a sack of stinky onions
right at the feet
of Brother Leo
"She is a liar!"
never looked
back when she
walked away

first domino fell
when mama walked
into his viciously
devised trap
and gave up
one of her children
voluntarily

CHAPTER 42 – Thread of Insanity

My scalp is tingling fire and my hair is hanging in my face

but I can see him
fat and bilious
triumphant
black, basilisk eyes
hard as marble
unmerciful
dark hair neatly
combed back
from his spongy
brown, pock
marked face

supple leather belt
goes on forever
around his immense
girth, holding up
meticulously
pressed brown pants
perfect crease
down the front
of each leg
over a spotless
white vee neck
tee-shirt

from my position
on the floor
I can see he wears
soft moccasin
slippers on his
puffy brown feet
so much
sparkling clean
over gloating

reptilian mean
wafting from him
the familiar
floral cologne
but today there
is more
a particular
satisfied aura
surrounds him
this is what
he has been
waiting for
today, I have
nowhere to hide
not even a veneer
of protection

today will be *bad*
I try to control
involuntary shivers
grit my teeth to stop
them chattering
my dress is ripped
and dirt smeared
knees and toes
skint, bloody bits
of dirt and gravel
ground into
fresh abrasions

peeking furtively
from the hair
hanging in my face
a trapped
animal-child
desperate for help
gaze slides by
older siblings
watching

silent, no help
I am all alone
he *knows* he can do
whatever he
wants to me
he leans down
puffing cinnamon
breath, voice soft
sibilant, menacing
"Your mother always had too much Phileo love. Today you have seen her Agape love."
he raised his
voice to orator
speaking
to the adults
as they walked
by me, to fill
their plates
"Pass by and look on this liar."

I did not see
pity or concern
they think I deserve this
maybe.... they
were afraid
didn't want
their kids to suffer
capitulation by silence
or entrenched
righteous vigor
"Spare the rod, spoil the child"

Brother Leo
calm, content
took his time
to preach an
impromptu sermon

"This child is corrupted, unless we help her, she will burn. Hell is a lake of fire where sinners burn forever. Children must understand what God expects of them. They must understand the fire. Take her Brother, show her what hell feels like."

lifted off the floor
by my brother
hauled to the burner
on the stove
my arm pulled
forward, anchored
under his elbow
cringing body
pressed into his
back, horrifying
backwards hug
that first sting
rising to
unbearable torment
don't know if
I screamed
I heard nothing
my other hand
thrashed and
clawed at his back
he let me go
when all four
of my fingers
suffered sufficiently
seared in the flames
of this hell, my life

near the table
laden with food
my brother parked
me on one of the
hated metal
folding chairs
told me not to move
as if I was not

morbidly distressed
quaking with fear
trying not to
anticipate the
abuses still to come

Brother Leo sat
in his large comfortable
chair, Sisters
quietly served him
contemplatively
chewing his food
he looked down
on me while
adults continued
to arrive, moved around
the buffet type table
choosing their meal
breaded elk steak
spiced yams
baked potatoes
roasted corn
noodle casserole
chocolate praline pie
sweet ice tea
and hot coffee
they filled plates
ignored me
bedraggled urchin

I understood
the monster was
crafting my penance
it wouldn't be
just another beating
I could take that
this would be worse
I felt for around for
the fizzy place

and the little girl who
wasn't me, couldn't
find her, no one to
inhabit this skin suit
but me, alone
softly like a snag
pulled on an old sweater
my mind began to unravel

dinner complete
Sisters supervised
assigned kids
to wash and towel dry
hundreds of dishes
pots and pans
clinking silverware
Brother Leo
watched from his chair
picking his teeth
my brother
sat next to him
waiting for orders

The Dining Hall
emptied slowly
until it was just me
alone with Brother Leo
and my brother
so handsome
wearing a
cowboy hat
and vest, over
a western shirt
finally, Brother Leo speaks

You will stay here tonight. In the morning you will be stripped naked and you will march the roads until our Lord Jesus forgives you. Do not move. The Lord will show me if you do."

ears pricked
"Stripped naked"
modesty gone
girl arms, knees
legs, supposed
to be covered
everything I knew
shattered

"Let your women adorn themselves in modest apparel, knees and arms covered as may become holiness."

stark imagery
me, naked, pale
imperfect, pudgy
secret places exposed
walking a gauntlet
of jeering adults
men, women
and other kids
gusting shame
pushed hard against
buttressed walls
my safe place was
in trouble

my brother squatted
on his heels in front of me
"Don't move from that chair. The Lord will show him if you do."
they turned off the lights
closed the doors
left me in the dark
with bloody toes
and throbbing
fingers, nerve
endings scalded
searing acid pain
I couldn't get away
from it, squeezed

my wrist hard
no relief, painful
lesson pounded to
the rhythm of my heart

with my uninjured hand
I reached to push
tangled hair
out of my face
a clump of hair
ripped from my scalp
came loose
drifted from
my fingers to the floor

Suffering in a cloak of stygian dark

I could see only the
tiny luminescent
hands of the clock
on the stove
at the far end
of The Dining Hall
all the shrieking
angst inside me
heightened for tomorrow
alone, in pain, terrified
I desperately
hoped this night
would last forever

most of the day
half the night
filled with fear
and panic, I
needed to pee
too afraid to move
heavy lassitude
stole into my limbs
I nodded off
slumped over in
the hard chair
drifted, dreamed

slowly stood
dream walked
away from the chair
felt my way
across the floor
up the steps
down the hall
into the bathroom
to the toilet
settled to release

the terrible tension
in my bladder

jerked awake
to remember
my troubles all
over again, now
I sat in a smelly
puddle of fear induced
pheromonal urine
dripping sound
a soft splash
on the linoleum

hazy epiphany
I would go crazy
my fortress was
not strong enough
for this insult
physical pain
plundered my heart
everything
hurt so bad, I
cradled throbbing
blistered fingers
against my chest
hot tears gushed again
"I want mama.... I want mama......I want mama."
once the words came
from me, I couldn't stop them
miserable sobbing mantra
echoed in the
dark empty Dining Hall

hours later, crashing
breakers, subsided to
numb exhaustion
I talked to Jesus
"If you are there and you can hear me, please, please, help me, don't let him do this."

fragile sanity uncertain and
soft, poised like a
dandelion puff
ready to spin away
in a light breeze

my brother returned
very early, released me
to run home to mama
burned, scabbed
barefoot, and torn
still damp with urine
fear eked from me
like bad poison
scrambled, heaving
but clear on one point
"Brother Leo said he would strip me naked, make me march up and down the roads."

mama shushed me
ran a warm bath
soothed my burns
with cold butter
picked up my torn
stinking clothes
and quietly left
likely she went to
The Dining Hall
cleaned up the urine
I left puddled on the
chair and the floor

I crawled into
bed, brain exhausted
body battered
throbbing hand
curled against my heart
hot thumping pain
inside and out
Esther, still asleep

curled into my back
our breath synchronized
sleep followed
momentary safety
achieved in
the cosmic spiral
of twin connectivity

unbearable tense fear
waiting at home
kept from school
terrified by every knock
on our door
days continued
with belly aching
anticipatory dread
Esther and I clung
sleep eluded
when I drifted
I dreamed, I saw
myself naked
alone, nothing to
cover me but
my shame
maybe God would
help me go to sleep
and never wake

the naked humiliation
did not happen
I'll never know
if mama made
a deal with the devil
or if sweet Jesus
from my toddler days
intervened to
spare my mind

My reprieve did not last long

summoned several
days later, advantage

taken while mama was
off kilter, another interrogation

the blisters on my fingers
wrinkled now, peeling

in waxy flakes from new
and tender pink skin

escorted into the brown
bathroom, no longer unusual

to be standing under his
obsidian lizard scrutiny

as he sat, on his brown toilet
toadstool, he knew I was there

right on the lip of fracture, causally
nudged me closer to no return

he held a polaroid picture
in front of me, pointed

"There, that's a devil coming out of your mouth."

the photo, snapped by Sister
Dorothy last Christmas

as the kids passed in a line
each one stopped to receive

a wrapped gift and brown bag of
goodies, me, hair in long curls

there, floating near my mouth
a tiny, curling, black edged bubble

still, I flinch for photos
always wonder what will

show itself, *"Photos can't lie"*
my discomfort is obvious

snared face always askew
off somehow, frozen oddness

and incomplete expression
mouth uncertain, waiting

a devil? I stared at him
vapid gaze, afraid to speak

he stared back, he knew
he had me, *"Are you ready to confess?"*

no longer sure of myself
I couldn't cling to ideas of

absolute right or wrong, truly
terrified, he would do whatever

took his demented fancy, decide
new ways to punish and confuse

fresh and dogged in my mind
the threat of stripping me naked

I understood, I must confess
what I have no memory of

I heard it all again, a litany
of sickening, sexual crimes

"Did you put your mouth on your brother's privates? Did your brothers play with your privates? Did you do nasty things to other little girls, did you put your fingers in their privates? who have you molested?"

he didn't ask when, where
or for how long

he didn't have to, I answered
"Yes" admitted all the nasty

in monotone, gave him
names, other little girls

playmates, nieces,
friends, anyone I could

wrangle from my twisted
tortured brain, many

names to ruin me
make me the evil thing

he believed me to be
induced, I sold my birthright

from my own mouth
gilded my future cage

bathroom door partially
open, now he swung it wide

to further complete my ruin
make me sure, I had no refuge

"Brother Ed come in here. Did you hear her confession?

daddy, strained, looking tired
older, and so sad, nodded

"Turn your face from her, my brother. This is not your daughter."

I stared at daddy, pleaded silently
please daddy, don't do it......grab me, squeeze me tight.... run away from here....

visibly shrinking, familiar broad hand
on the counter, he leaned hard into

the brown marble surface, his
upper body reflected in the mirror

daddy stared at me with red rimmed eyes
oddly, with tenderness I'd never

seen, Brother Leo placed a hand on his
cheek, gave a slight push, I watched daddy

and his reflection turn away from me
desolation swept over me

a hot stinging wind, daddy kept
his face turned, head down

Brother Leo talked of his intentions
"I am removing her from your home permanently. You are old parents with too much Phileo love and you have allowed evil to grow in your offspring, you are not Godly enough to recognize the growing threat, the evil seed. Brother Branham charged me to be your leader, your shepherd."

defeated, daddy left the
bathroom, head lowered

I only saw glimpses of him
for years after, labeled

a deviant sexual predator
at the tender age of nine

"disfellowshipped"
from all in The Park

forbidden to speak
with other children

shunned, no partaking in
activities arranged for

the children, all required to
turn their face from me

I would be, *"shorn like a lesbian"*
still wasn't sure what a lesbian was

but I understood, *"shorn"* so
I knew what was coming

Brother Leo informed me about lesbians
"Women, who dress like men, and lick each other's privates like dogs."

I internalized this vulgarity
he enhanced my ignorance

using the derogatory and gross
informed my growing mind

in ways that would wreck me for
years to come, daddy's betrayal

dragged at my soul, ripped
my heart open to elemental

loss, frustration, and rage, bitterly
moored in a place beyond time

Brother Leo's denunciation settled
in my heart and belly like greasy suet

"No man will ever want you. No man will ever love you. You will never satisfy a man. You will never give a man authority over you. This is required by God."

words to weaken the bones of
my future, to haunt me as I learned

and acquired carnal knowledge
in that moment I understood

only, that privates are nasty
not even a qualification

for their use as areas
for physical elimination

silently, I stood and waited
caged in the shit brown bathroom

phased out, glazed over, if
I was too tired to fear him

he was useless, he concluded
his reproof, called for my brother

to walk me up the cobbled flagstone
sidewalk into the barber shoppe

located behind Brother Ron
and Sister Margie's trailer

Brother Carl, the men's barber
waited there, again he had been

told what to do, he led me
zombie like, to the barber chair

novelty for any girl child to
be sitting there for a haircut

he shook out a long cloth drape
fastened it around my neck

I focused on the deep cleft
like a skin canyon, in his chin

he did not look at me
craggy old face, emotionless

no sympathy noted
in spite of his own beliefs

he would cut my hair off
for the *second* time I would be

an abomination before God
my family, and my community

"Serpent's Seed"

CHAPTER 43 – Second Shearing

Brother Carl pulled my hair back in a tail

before he cut it off
dropped it on the floor
light brown, limp
disconnected
from living roots
drifting like down
at the base
of the barber chair
words of the Prophet
thundered in
my head, absolute

"The glory of a woman is in her hair." And you've cut yours off. What was it? It was her glory. The only decent thing she had about her was her long hair. Bobbed haired women, not worth a good clean bullet to kill them with it."

he gave me a radical
haircut, as directed
pulled my hair
upward in a comb

snip…snip…....snip
shame…. shame……...shame

flights of hair
rained around me
lost feathers
spiraling to the floor
now, electric clippers buzzing
would he shave me bald?
buzzed over my ears
pushed my head
down, shaved
the back of my neck
finished, he stood back

spun me around
flashing past
onlookers in the door
I was a comedy, they
enjoyed my shame
while they played a game
chin rubbing, pointing
my brother, his wife
among them

"Which boy does she look the most like?"
"Hmm, what do you think?"
"She doesn't really look like Johnny or Tony."

ridicule sizzled
could not catch flame
I had no tinder left
they began to name boys
around my age
consensus reached
my brother's wife
in her musical voice
"It's James, she looks just like James!"

ridiculous sight
homemade dress
jarhead haircut
a thing to laugh at
"She looks like a boy in a dress."

handed a broom
and dustpan, I swept
up my glory
threw it in the
garbage
hardly tears
just more
briny water
falling from

my face, bits
of chopped hair
stuck in the runnels

leaden fatigue
in my heart, but
the bloody muscle
just continued to bang
a tired thumping rhythm

lub dub….shame….shame…

numbly resigned to
to my beating
for the day
couldn't get away
couldn't worry, or care
what came next
I would be told
what to do
I wanted mama
and Esther, but
I was too tired
to hold onto
the need, a
purple thistle
caught in
a wind storm of
commands
I dared not question

spinning, I would
land where I
landed, everything
felt distant
inside I was
powerless
almost serene
just waiting

for instructions
abandonment
accepted
no help from
parents, siblings
or Jesus

CHAPTER 44 – Brother Herb and Sister Grace

So, here I am

delivered to the
door of the Canadians
depleted, brain dead
a note in my hand
unsure what it says
but accustomed to
my iniquities
placed in writing
carrying everything
I own stuffed
in a garbage bag
hair buzzed off
and a multitude of
new throbbing welts
and bruises on
back, butt, and legs

at least no one
is shooting me
with word arrows
barbed, to lodge
deep in the tender
flesh of my heart
and mind, I am
already pierced
like Saint Sebastian
bristling with arrows
but breathing still

Sister Grace
answers the door
a smallish lady
with ashy blonde hair
in a smooth chignon

wearing a neat pencil skirt
takes the note
invites me in
allows me to sit
in a beautiful
brocaded chair
she sits down
on her couch
ultra-ladylike
knees modestly
covered, she
unseals the note
and reads it
gazes at me, reads
it again, her face
all sharp angles
but not unkind
looks me over
again, takes in the
garbage bag at my feet

their home is
unlike anything
I've seen before
a trailer but very
different from ours
sculptures, maybe Chinese
strange artifacts
and artwork
things I've only
seen in books

right out on the
coffee table
a large hardcovered
book, with a
great beautiful building
arches, curves, twists
colored domes

golden spires
incredible fairytale
architecture
my eyes drift across
the word *"Leningrad"*

sluggish awareness
creates a weird
warped sense of time
my gaze slips to
another colorful
multipage book
of butterflies

my head turns
slowly of its own
accord, tracking
I see more books
of course, the Bible
The Seven Church Ages
National Geographic
magazines, notable
yellow rimmed, with
exotic photographs
stacks of books
thick and heavy
I cannot see titles
even exhausted
demoralized as I am
rising in me a familiar
tingle of need

beneath worn
raggedy shoes
pale green carpet
like summer melon
and displayed on either
end of a long
beautifully carved

table, two golden
gleaming, spouted urns
I would later learn
are called *"Samovars"*
so much intricate
foreign beauty
right in front of me
like someone else's story

Sister Grace purses her lips
clucks her tongue
looks at me again
seems to make
a decision
asks if I'd like
to take a nap
I nod without speaking
she leads me to
a small room
with a little bed
neatly made
everything
smells different
no hints of
oatmeal, fried eggs
bacon or beans
a light exotic scent
unfamiliar to me
everything
unreal, dreamlike

she turns down
the covers, allows
me to crawl in
fully clothed
old shoes abandoned
on the floor
beside my garbage bag
welcome escape

drifting into
the minimally safe
world I knew, sleep

woke to the sound
of muffled voices
stay curled up
in the little bed
secure, snugged
in the blanket, not sure
what happens next

very late afternoon
the sliding door
opens, Sister Grace
quietly asks if I'd
like something
to eat, invited
to sit at their small
kitchen table

already there
sitting, Brother Herb
"Welcome Deborah"
large homely bald man
solemn eyes behind
thick horn-rimmed glasses
calm measured voice
Sister Grace
wearing a perfectly
pressed apron
slicing fruit
at the counter

"You are going to be staying with us for a while. Do you like tea?"

on the table
a squatty black
iron teapot

steam curling
from the spout
I've never had tea
sometimes mama
gives us coffee
with lots of milk
and sugar
he fills a gaping void
with new knowledge
"The secret of tea, is timing. The water must be boiling when it is added to the tea, and it must steep for the exact amount of time. Tea is all about ceremony and contemplation. It must never be rushed."

I noted fragile
China teacups
with golden rims
twining delicate roses
filigree handles
like little ears
sitting atop
matching saucers
Sister Grace
places a plate
on the table
odd little triangles
of dark brown
toasted bread
tiny pats of butter

Brother Herb
shakes out a
cloth napkin, I
pick mine up
do the same
place it carefully
in my lap, he
pours steaming
tea into my cup
"Careful now, it's very hot"

I can smell
spices, oranges
woody and strange
haven't blessed
the food yet
not sure what
to do next, I wait
Sister Grace
joins us at the table
Brother Herb
bows his head
blesses the food

she adds a sweep
of brown jelly
"Fig preserves"
places it on
my plate, not sure
what a fig is
stomach rumbles
still, I wait for
them to start
then I devour mine
like a starving dog
buttery sweet
odd popping seeds
Sister Grace
immediately
places another one
on my plate

carefully, I puff
and sip tea, a burst
of misty flavors
over my lips and tongue
but no sweetness
Brother Herb
offers me a dish
of sugar cubes

a tiny pair of tongs
"*Normally, good tea doesn't need sugar, but you may have some if you like.*"

subtly, the world
brightened
I'd just eaten
things I didn't
know existed
drank hot tea with
a very graceful
English influenced
childless couple
treated me
carefully as
fragile bone China

This is why I believe in God today

he noted my despair
and drifting sanity
these two people
recognized an
almost broken child
and very softly
they became my world
fortressed my hungry
mind with information
books, experiences
and treasures, some
I still own today

they could not protect
me completely from
Brother Leo's machinations
but they gave what they could
I loved them beyond
belief, my life with them
was fairytale wonderful until
The Servant of the Lord
figured it out
and crushed all of us

Esther and I were to be
separated almost
completely for
the next four years
all five of us were taken
from daddy and mama
moved into different homes
our lives, our actions
carefully monitored
I was *"disfellowshipped"*
and shunned but

miraculously given the gift of
Brother Herb and Sister Grace
for a little while

Sister Grace pulled clothing out of the crumpled garbage bag

helped me sort
out a few worn
dresses and underwear
socks with mama's
neat stitching
visible at the
heels and toes

we moved some
boxes out of
the little room
hung my few
dresses in the
closet and put
folded undies and socks
in the drawers below
my single pair
of shoes went
under the chair
by the door
"I think you need some new clothes for school."

school, the thought
of Monday
made me hollow
half-way through
fourth grade
how would I bear
the cruel words
and actions of
other children?
they already called us
"weirdos" and *"Jesus freaks"*
what would they
call me now?
I had never known
a day at school

when someone wasn't
mocking or poking fun
as a group, this
was easier to take
but the day after
tomorrow
I would be
walking alone
separated
shamed at home
and at school

I said nothing
but Sister Grace
noted my distress
"I'll walk you to school on Monday."
she showed me where
to put my toothbrush
in their beautiful
blue bathroom
pristine seashells
unlike any I'd ever
seen, on the counter
and the back of the toilet

fresh bathwater
all to myself
she sprinkled in
little crystals
dissolved into
sweet smelling
bubbles, left me to
undress and soak in the
warm water, I sank
down until water
ringed my face
submerged, my ears
thumped in sync
with my heart

I stayed until
it got cold, dried off
carefully dressed
in night clothes

remotely curious
I looked into the mirror
wanted to see
the devil in my mouth
slow motion, I touched
my face, under my fingers
ordinary pale skin
light spray of freckles
across my nose and cheeks
blue eyes stared back
no warty red devil skin
I rubbed my hands
over light brown spiky hair
bare ears and neck
no budding black horns
opened my mouth
lifted my tongue
searched beneath
just watery and pink
little blue veins
twisted up into the
back of my tongue

pulled my cheeks
out with hooked
fingers, inspected
teeth and gums
I could not see a
devil lurking there
but I was still certain
there was no place in the
Kingdom of Heaven
for me, no rest in God's peace
for a little girl harboring

unseen devils
I didn't like who
I saw in the mirror
a puny, helpless liar
I began to avoid
mirrors and cameras
after that day

Struggling, struggling, breathlessly frightened, trying to avoid the strong hands

gripping my arms, I hear
the snap and whack of leather

my skin wobbles, warps
and circular belt welts

writhe up, freed
from abused flesh

to turn and snap at
me, striking serpents

inflicting fiery pain
desperately I wrench

both arms free, cover
my head but they

strike, like ice picks
through my scalp

sweat trickles
from my hairline

I wake panicked
jerked from agonizing

night terrors, fingers
scrabbling on my head

seeking my long hair
it's gone, it's really gone

post traumatic nightmare
the first of many

sleep is no longer

a safe place for me

fully awake now
eyes squeezed shut

I hear a tiny chiming
muted and sweet

a fairy bell under glass
I let my eyes

flutter open
a different ceiling

different bed
new smells, again

the tiny chime
barefoot, I sneak

out the door
pulled along, lightly

stepping, hesitant
a curious rabbit

led by the dulcet
sterling chime

I find the clock
ornate and curvy

tiny key sitting
in a dish before it

I absorb every
detail, still in

my nightgown

hands at my sides

I move around
the sitting room

seeing everything
with hungry eyes

stopped in front
of the great book

of butterflies
"Would you like to look at it?"

startled, I look up
to see Brother Herb

in his belted robe
tea cup in hand

he places the book
into my lap, time is

slow, I am dissolving
serenely dazed, gently

I finger page after
page of delicate silken

butterflies, orange
tiger striped mystery

iridescent fairy purple
swallow tailed flight

gliding blue coquet
tiny red and black

chitin, swirling beauty
all emerged from

ordinary, even ugly
chrysalis to transformation

and a new beginning

Sunday, they chose to forgo breakfast at The Dining Hall

Sister Grace prepared
stewed prunes
and poached eggs
I didn't like them
but ate anyway
mama fried eggs hard
put em on biscuits

quietly, they informed
me of house rules
homework after school
bedtime at 830pm
read any books
I like, as long as I
treat them respectfully
wash my hands first

Sister Grace washed dishes
while Brother Herb
inquired about things I liked
he did not mention
my status as a liar
and sexual deviant
said nothing about
anyone's *privates*

hesitantly, a few words
at a time, he coaxed
from me, my love for the
battered orange
books in the
school library
biographies of
famous people and
the great chiefs
he listened attentively
while I spilled out

my obsession
the ways of the
Indians, Americas
indigenous tribes
I felt my face redden
when I told him
my secret, I thought
I might belong
with them

I could imagine
Cynthia Ann Parker
captured as a child
around my age
married into the tribe
she had a son
the famous
Quanah Parker
she did not want to
leave the world
she had grown
to love more
than her own

Though I was living with Brother Herb and Sister Grace, I was

still required
to eat dinner at
The Toddle House
seated alone
away from
other children
I saw Esther
across the room
sitting with Sharon
knew they and
Johnny and Tony
had been taken from
daddy and mama
were now living in
different homes

I suffered a
distinct snapping
disconnect
I was no one
belonged to no one
my heart ached with the
painful ripping
loneliness
of being unlike others
I did not fit, not
even with the weirdos
and Jesus freaks
in our commune

Cut out of the pack

a straggler, forced
to walk alone
to and from school
an aberration entrenched
among the aberrant
interaction with
Park kids forbidden
vulnerability spiced the
wind, pheromonal
whiff of the rejected

prey

for a skinny bully, his
own angst demonstrated
in hair twirling
while sitting in class
gathered minions
other misfits, who
with some prodding

hunt

torment weaker kids
mean spirited brats
rarely act alone
three moved behind me
snide, menacing
"Is that a pixie haircut, Jesus freak?"

fear

walking, defenseless
terrified more of
spectacle and ridicule
knew they could not
match my prior
experience with

pain

jeering, poking
grabbing at
the books I clutched
to my chest
the three started
with growing fervor
to kick me in the butt
all the way down
Gurley street

humiliation

I didn't speak
no screaming
no running
no attempt to
protect myself
ducked my head
kept walking
face flaming
accustomed to

shame

chose to endure
the assault
curled around my books
jolted forward
on the end of
brutal shoes
cars passing
must have seen
a strange little girl
in a long dress
with a jarhead haircut
pursued by

school yard bullies
kicked down
the sidewalk
like an empty can

no one stopped
no one rolled
down a window
no one hollered
"Stop that!"
completely
cruelly *alone*
the three kicked me
right up to the sign
at the entrance of
Pine Lawn Trailer Ranch
before releasing me
from their pointy

demons

no Jesus
no good Samaritans
no police officers
no teachers
no parents
no siblings
no friends

no tribe

just new fiends
to rule over my life
my every breath
all of them somehow
blessed by God
given allowance
to persecute
disfellowshipped

tomorrow
there would be more
and I would live to
endure another day

I slip quietly into the house

close the door behind me
my heart bumps
around my ribcage
a nervous gerbil
running from one
snare to another
anticipating ruin

I close my eyes
take a deep breath in
let it out slowly, feel
a bit of serenity and
hope, after the first
weeks in my new
surroundings
I know I will find a snack
on the table, little
poppy seed crackers
pickled cabbage
cream cheese
tea biscuits

still adjusting
to Brother Herb
and Sister Grace
amazed, grateful
for such gentle care
they don't seem to
realize that I am
a deviant, named as
"Serpent's Seed"
such strange adults
talked with me
waited for my reactions
let me answer honestly
as if my brain
works and my heart

is not a chunk
of cracked granite

I carry my things down
the hall to my room
slide the door open
latest troubles
immediately forgotten
a beautiful coverlet
intricate Native design
is draped over my bed
walls redone in pale
yellow and white
striped wallpaper
an authentic beaded
papoose board
hangs on the wall
along with a beaded
buckskin shirt
and a framed picture
of an Indian Village
on a peaceful
river bank, horses
grazing in the tall grass

eyes roving, I register
the import of this event
they heard me and have
done this just for me
adults *listened* to
what I said, and it
mattered enough
to create this
wonderful village
from my dreams
maybe they really care
about my thoughts
the burn of tears
prickles behind

my eyelids
my throat feels
thick and hot
I don't know what to say
I can only show them

That evening when I returned

from dinner at
The Toddle House
there was more
Brother Herb
presented to me
paper wrapped
drinking glasses
six of them
each embossed
with a picture of one
of the Great Chiefs
I would earn them
one at a time
every few months
if I got good grades
and did my chores

Saturday mornings
still required to go
to work separately
not allowed to
join in chores or play
with the other kids
otherwise, Sister Grace
kept me occupied
sat me down at her sewing
machine and taught
me to make
little neck pillows
carefully stuffed
a cloth carrying loop
tucked into the
the end and neatly
hand stitched
I made one
start to finish by
myself, she let me

take it to mama
she showed me
neat folds of fabric
for new dresses. allowed
me to pick the colors
dark green with tiny blue
and purple flowers
another light blue with
yellow blossoms
finally pale pink with
with thin white stripes

measured and turned
nape to hemline
she would take these
to Sister Connie, to sew
dresses for me
we picked out socks
at Pennington's
she, shocked
at my large feet
for a nine-year-old
could find nothing that fit
"We'll get shoes next week."

Brother Herb
loved his garden
encouraged me to
help him carry pavers
and decide where the path
would wind, together
we planted an
Evening Primrose
enjoyed many summer
evenings, sipping tea
as we watched the
yellow blooms
unfurl and erupt
to full flower

each like a miniature
sunset in the dusk
we hiked through
the rocky boulders
by the running creek
he pointed out plants
and trees, my favorite
the bountiful
Manzanita bush
with its glossy smooth
blood red branches
dark green leaves
and seasonal red berries
life settled into
a rhythm, gradually
I began to trust them
and accept
my current
circumstances

CHAPTER 45 – Invictus

Hidden, in an obscure corner

of the school library
a section I was not
supposed to be in
reserved for older kids
a book of poetry
first experience with
rhythm and rhyme
profound verse
not biblical but
resonant, breathtaking
a life experience recorded
on fragile paper
in black and white, words
to be light rimmed
in my forever

Out of the night that covers me
black as the pit from pole to pole
I thank whatever Gods may be
for my unconquerable soul

In the fell clutch of circumstance
I have not winced or cried aloud
under the bludgeonings of chance
my head is bloody but unbowed

Beyond this place of wrath and tears
looms but the horror of the shade
and yet the menace of the years
finds, and shall find me unafraid

It matters not how straight the gate
how charged with punishments the scroll
I am the master of my fate!

I am the captain of my soul!

written nearly
one hundred years ago
impacted like an avalanche
who was this person
speaking my pain
ripe and raw?

who navigated the
straight and narrow gate
suffered vilification
and judgement
rose up from a
mangled soul to see
a confident path
through the murk
of a dictated life?
William Ernest Henley

I felt some guilty misgiving
at the mention
of *"Gods"* rather
than *"God"*
doubtful questions
on my teachings that
Jesus is my co-pilot
my life, my breath
my soul, my entire being

but the words of
the Prophet
always thrumming
in my subconscious mind
unprompted
streamed like a banner
filling the scarlet
space behind my eyes

"When the deep is calling to the deep, out there from God in his universe, there has got to be a deep to respond to it."

this, my deep calling
I had never read words
leapt in my being
coiled like a live wire
around my ever
hardening heart
spoke to me
of endurance
and determination

I felt a similar twinge
of conscience when
I read aloud
*"I am the master of my fate!
I am the captain of my soul!"*
but that ringing
intelligence became
a hard constant
my anchor
the succor of those words
dripped into my wounds
trickled over
ridges and scars
created in me
the will to survive
meaningful as
the, *"Balm in Gilead"*

I carried them with
me into my future
ironically tucked
in the pages
of my Bible, from
pocket to purse
or framed on the wall
this enlightenment

more precious
than any words
so far, from
Genesis to Revelations

CHAPTER 46 - Panda

There was room for one more in our world of three

habitually, I endured
school, and upon returning
home in the afternoons
placed my jacket
and shoes in my room
as a matter of habit
moved to the kitchen
to have a snack
do my homework
this routine was comfortable
I felt somewhat safe

had two or three new dresses
but continued to avoid
looking in the mirror
I could never unsee
the shame of
my cropped hair
and sneaky demons
Sister Grace
bought me plastic
headbands to push
through my hair so
I could pretend
I still had a ponytail

awesome afternoon
when I came home
from school to find a
strip of plywood
set upright between
the kitchen and
the living room
from behind it an

unmistakable whimper
a tiny fluffy tail
waving like a flag
just beyond the
wooden barrier
a brown and white
puppy, bounded up
up on short hind legs
perfectly round
black spots
covered bright eyes
peeking over the barrier

I picked him up and
sprawled on the floor
arms full of excited
wriggling puppy
bouncing, snarfing
haurrr, rruaf!
licking my face
I snuggled him
close, undisturbed
by poo on his feet

homework ignored
I was still sitting there
when Sister Grace
came in, busily
began mopping up
pees and poops
on the kitchen linoleum
wiping poo off
puppy paws, directed
me to change my clothes
clucking her tongue
"Herb brought him home at lunch today, but I don't know about a dog in the house."
noted my radiant
hopeful infatuation
and like a mama

she caved

name for this
sweet excited dandy
a daily discussion
Geronimo, Sequoia
Cochise, Bandit
Ranger, Outlaw, Chief?
on the coffee table
a magazine
glossy photograph
on the front, a
rotund Asian bear
munching bamboo
two perfect circles
surrounding
shiny black eyes
a total likeness
we named
our puppy *Panda*

excommunication
stopped hurting
so much, safely
ensconced in
this new home
training a new puppy
walking, bathing
brushing him
carefully measuring
food into bowls
kept me occupied
entertained

in time the ache
of losing Esther
dimmed and I
found new joys

in the world
of discussion, reason
and a new puppy

CHAPTER 47 – Embracing a New Life

Brother Herb let me offer my opinions

freely, steered
me to think wisely
separate each
component in a book
dissect and learn
he introduced me
to the *Knights*
of the Round Table
St George and the Dragon
Ivanhoe, Siegfried
Hamlet and Ophelia
Othello, and King Lear's daughters
multiplication tables
came easily, though
I did not like math
he never got
angry with me, but
behind his glasses
his eyes would bulge
a little, the only notable
agitation when teaching
me long division

I struggled with
book reports
wanted to rewrite
the whole story
with great patience
he taught me summary
and synopsis
I leeched stability
and inspiration from
his large sincere
presence, lumpy

unhandsome
utterly wonderful

a glorious foodie, he
loved to eat new things
after a lengthy
discussion about
American Indians and how
they used every scrap of
the buffalo they hunted
he came home
with large beef bones
still pinkish and
bloody, sawed into
short lengths
"Do you see anything here you can eat?"
mystified negative
"Oh, but there is"

the bones went into
salted boiling water
impromptu lesson on
the benefits of
bone marrow as
we scooped savory
broth flavored
greyish mush
out of the bones
and spread it
on buttered bread

I tried so many
new things to eat
my very first lobster
Russian caviar on
Lahvosh crackers
pickled daikon
smoked salmon
with capers

even edible flowers
the joy of using
all of my senses to
experience new things
so far, unequaled

Brother Herb
took me rummaging
through flea markets
and thrift stores
he had an eye for elegance
hidden in dusty corners
and old bins, Celadon
bowls and vases
carved jade jars

we happened upon
a wonderful stack of
soft magazine style
comic books
took the whole pile
Illustrated Classics
fodder for the future

2000 Leagues Under the Sea
Moby Dick, Robin Hood,
Wuthering Heights, Jane Eyre
Little Women, Huckleberry Finn
Call of The Wild, Great Expectations
Grapes of Wrath, The Secret Garden

a hundred opportunities
in hundreds of pages
fluttering promises
preserved for the day
I could enlist them in my service

I was beginning to feel safe, relaxed, and happy

when a package arrived
carried by one of
Brother Leo's minions
attached, a note
for Sister Grace
instructions to make
clothes for me
using the material
and the pattern enclosed
included, a viciously
barbed word arrow
"Clothing appropriate for a lesbian"
Sister Grace said nothing
clucked her tongue
clenched her jaw

tweedy, woolen
big yellow and black
squares, not plaid
but checkerboard
Butterick pattern equally
awful, a masculine
suit coat, straight skirt
completed the look
androgynous, elderly
I was to wear it
for school pictures

speechless, trapped
nothing I could do
Sister Grace tried
to dainty it up
chose a white blouse
ruffled at the neck
resigned, I dressed
buttoned and zipped
stuffed into an

ugly casing like
a Victorian sausage

I walked carefully
skirt bound me
from waist to knees
jacket equally binding
long sleeved, scratchy
mummification
for a living child
Brother Leo's way
of letting me know
he could touch me
anytime

my life at school
became worse
obediently, I wore it
endured recess and activities
unable to move freely
I sat alone, watching
dodge ball, and
hopscotch
my face red and hot
but no longer
willing to shed tears
internalized this humiliation
the way I always did
other kids, forever
ready to pounce

"Hey Granny Grunt, are you ten or a hundred and ten?"

"Ohhhhh, she's gonna cry!"

cruel childish laughter
a thrown dodgeball
hit me in the shoulder
bounced into

my face, knocked
my glasses off my face
to the ground

"Go on Granny Grunt, pick up your glasses!"

forced to move
no longer able to
take refuge in
in silent immobility
required to bend over
pick them up, settle
them back on my face
stupidly graceless

"Granny, Granny, Granny Grunt! Got your glasses, where's your cane?"

complete and total misery
until the bell rang
I dreaded seeing
those pictures
my shame immortalized
always weird in
front of cameras
my excruciating
oddness
emphasized
brutal truth
a very cruel lens

brown cropped hair
Dippity Do'd
scraped back with
an incongruous
plastic headband
too small glasses
white ruffled collar
bursting from
a checkered

androgenous suit
the colors of a
yellow and black
race pennant

Ignorance is bliss

the US had been in a
state of unrest for years
conflict was the
word of the day
Haight Ashbury love-in's
and the rise of LSD
1967 *"Summer of Love"*
punctuated by fulminant
and violent social unrest
Watts riots, Berkley protests
Kent State students
shot by National Guardsman
military personnel carriers
in the streets of America
more than 2000
stores and buildings
burned and looted
Martin Luther King
and Bobby Kennedy
assassinated within a few
months of each other
the Charles Mason cult
knife murders
and Helter Skelter

I was a listener
ears always attuned
but I never heard any of it
had a brother in the Army
though he went AWOL to stay
out of Vietnam, served his
time in Leavenworth
by 1971 we were
nearing the end of the
Vietnam war
school girls sold
POW bracelets

the way Girl Scouts
sell cookies
but exclusivity
was complete in the
bubble of our cultish life
we fit the definition of
a group of adherents
with great and fixed devotion
to a charismatic leader
no radio, no television
or even telephones
we lived by a set
of rigid guidelines
complete obedience
enforced by fervent followers
and fear of eternal
damnation

never saw a newspaper
my knowledge
completely limited
to the words
of the Prophet and
The Servant of The Lord
the most emphatic message
for young people
in my world The Beatles
were agents of Satan
Elvis sold his birthright
for a pot of gold

strangely enough
I have no memory
of education
or elucidation
concerning the war
and its causes
at school either
Prescott was a small

rural community of
approximately 13,000
folks wanted to
keep it that way
there was plenty
of mean to go around
always, school was
like grasping nettles
prepared for the burning
torment of the day
I resigned myself
to nasty jibes
and bullying
endured all
silently, impatiently
eyes on the clock
waiting for the
release bell

until I could
hot foot it home
to my saviors and Panda
always ready for
new delights
or old treasures
unwrapped
and presented
as a matter
of adventure
and opportunity
to expand my mind
beyond the
boundaries, both real
and metaphysical
surrounding The Park

The school year ended and summer break

started with another
reward of a glass to add
to the shelf in my room
where three of them stood
those inscrutable chiefs
looking over my tiny haven

my tenth birthday
was coming, I had
no expectations
but a note arrived
Sister Grace read it
eagerly happy
to inform me
I was allowed to go to
the afternoon movie at
The Dining Hall
initially I was shocked
then elated

I washed up
changed my clothes
brushed my hair
pushed a plastic
head band on
to hold growing
wisps of light brown
hair out of my face
movie started
at one o'clock

I arrived, tense
excited, feeling
out of place
my note viewed
by the projectionist
I was directed

to my chair
tables had been
removed and the
chairs were lined
in neat rows
excitement faded
in the second or two
it took for me to
realize my chair was
turned backwards
sitting near the
projector to ensure
obedience to
psychological torture

pointedly ignored
by the other kids
I listened to the
long overture
followed by a
bouncing tune
and male singers
shouting *"Jumbo"*
a deep male
voice, somehow
familiar, quite sure
it was Masala, the
bad Roman from *"Ben Hur"*

clanging tandem
of sledge hammers
working men sang
putting up a circus tent
"Get em sunk, mash em down, raise that canvas, pull it tight"
imagined sweaty
men, earning a hard
living, pounding tent
stakes, hauling manure
feeding lions

and tigers, all for
the ultimate show
a busted circus
gambling old pop
and his dutiful
daughter, keeping bill
collectors at bay and singing
"Swing high, swing low upon the trapeze, a year from now you'll do it with ease, to reach the top you gotta keep trying over and over and over again"

resigned, I closed
my eyes, tried to *see*
the parade, colorful and
exciting, winding through
the streets of a small town
clowns and acrobats
singing, shouting to the people
"Come to the circus"
at least I could
listen to the songs
and imagine a beautiful
lady in feathers
and a sparkling gown
riding the elephant
"Jumbo" star of
the Wonder Circus

later, hearing about it
Sister Grace seemed
annoyed, clucked her tongue
but said nothing
she and Brother Herb
had been busy
planning my birthday
lemon poppy seed cake
and my first fondue
in a little round electric
pot, using long
forks we plunged

chunks of beef
and pork into boiling oil
ate them with greens
and fresh brown bread

I unwrapped presents
they selected for me
a paint by number kit
two new books
and a bead loom
with tubes of
brightly colored
trade beads
Brother Herb
and I sat up late
and figured out
how to string it
and make clever
beaded bands with
a Native design

I went to bed happy
tired in a good way
acceptance of the
backwards movie
as my lot, knew there
would be more
and didn't care
slept, deeply satisfied
with a serene
new secret
my enchanted life
in its obscurity
somewhat safe
from Brother Leo
fuzzily unsure
how it happened

CHAPTER 48 – The Classics

My new books, an introduction

to the classics
"Les Misérables" and
"Count of Monte Christo"
profoundly affected
by the injustices
and suffering
of Jean Valjean
equally affected
by the revenge saga
of Edmond Dantes
lengthy discourse
with Brother Herb
about the power
of forgiveness
versus satisfaction
of revenge, he
quietly, emphatically
folded both into
my future mind
and like perfect
tea, let them steep

I still suffered
abuse at school
disfellowshipped
from the other kids
occasionally summoned
to sit backwards
in Saturday movies
completed lonely chores
and required Bible reading
Panda slept by my bed
I read and dialoged
with Brother Herb

like Jean Valjean
I loved my books

"Those undemanding but faithful friends."

I started 5th grade and sometimes I saw Esther when she was

with the other children
I never saw daddy
every now and then
I would sneak
around the back
over the rocks
across to the opposite
side of The Park
to the old blue
and white trailer
where daddy and
mama lived
without any of
their younger children

the door was never
locked, I could
walk in, most days
to find mama
lying on her side
asleep on the couch
under her neck
the little pillow I made
hard to rouse
so tired all the time
sometimes she
would open her eyes
see me sitting cross
legged, in front of her
whispered softly
"Debbie Dee,"
before drifting
back to sleep

I would sit silently
looking into her face
flummoxed by mixed

emotions, weighty love
and helpless pity
noted the lines
in her forehead
very lightly brushed
my fingers down
her soft cheek
gently pushed a strand
of grey hair
under her headscarf
watched her breathe
little puffing snores
poorly fitted
false teeth clacking
when her mouth relaxed

usually, I snuck out
the same way
I snuck in
don't know if
mama remembered
those times
or if they were
lost dreams

CHAPTER 49 – No Resistance

I heard daddy was in the hospital for

surgery, *"Ruptured gallbladder"*
didn't know
until years later
what really happened
abdominal trauma
like *"Ruptured spleen"*

Sister Joan had
one of her fits
daddy, in his usual
way, made a comment
"It's just the devil!"
something we all
heard everyone say
even witnessed attempts
to drive devils out of her
but her uncles, already
mad at daddy over
some tires they
bought from him
took offense, assaulted
him on his own patio

daddy was never
put off by a fight
or threat of violent action
even in his 50's
he'd be formidable
if he saw it coming

daddy always hit first

I was sure they
snookered him
got the drop on him
but Johnny was there
daddy didn't fight back
he let them beat
the ever-lovin tar
out of him
they shoved those
dirty old tires
over his head
and shoulders
pinned his arms
to his sides, so he
couldn't fight back
beat him like
a chained dog
kicked him the
head, belly, and groin
left him laying
on the patio

after surgery
he had a red
ridged scar down the
middle of his belly
daddy never
talked about it
I wonder
if he was ashamed
so many things
got out of his control
or just like mama
they broke him too

it caused a ripple
in my family
heard my oldest
brother got his rifle
was going after
them, his wife
talked him down
walked him, fuming
round and round
in circles for
most of the night

long standing
rivalry turned into
a real hard rift
between the
two families
lasted for years
uneasy truces
waxed and waned
this was a significant
issue, we had family
married into theirs
lasted even
after The Park
when the cult we built
broke apart like a
worm riddled vessel
drifted on the tides
of the past
along with
the multitude
of things we
did not speak of

CHAPTER 50 – Christmas Magic

Christmas 1971 came with a crisp cool wind and a

smattering of snow
walking distance from
The Park, a favorite landmark
Prescott Courthouse Square
always brightly
festive, a winking
mirage of lights
reflected in the
rain damp streets
an upside down
holiday square
pulsing with
joie de vivre and
season happy folks
late shopping
bands and music

joy of Christmas
uncelebrated in The Park
Jesus was not
born in December
but in the spring
"When nature brings forth baby lambs"
distinctly April
this *"Pagan"* holiday
shunned, considered wicked
the decorating of
trees, idolatrous

daddy always bought
marked down
toys and candy
after the holidays
but he maintained

a hard line, Christmas
would not be discussed
or celebrated in any way
in spite of these
teachings, my first
Christmas with
Herb and Grace
was beyond special
full of magic
and never before
experiences

tiny lights strung
surreptitiously, on
a small potted tree
inside the house
daily they placed
small wrapped presents
around it, enjoying
the anticipatory glee
each day built to
giddy excitement
delighted impatience

after dark we
went downtown
to enjoy the lights
and do some
Christmas shopping
something I had never
done, on either side
of me, Herb and Grace
held my hands as we walked
I was snugly bundled
in scarf and gloves and a
new knitted hat, something
they called a *"Tuque"*
bursting with excitement
filled with a kind of

joy I'd never felt before
enveloped by the
sights and sounds
of Christmas
we drank hot chocolate
with tiny mint flavored
marshmallows
as we meandered
Prescott's famous
Whiskey Row

quaint shops open late
glittering wares
arranged with canny
precision and grace
in brightly illuminated
display windows
everyone seemed
ethereal, smiles looked
real, I felt light inside
wound up with infectious cheer
our goal, a Christmas
gift for mama

we looked at gloves
scarves and brooches
ranged from store to store
Brother Herb
in his gentle way
making suggestions
pointing out possibilities
we settled on a necklace
of very light blue
graduated crystals
placed them
in a little wooden box
of polished maple
mother of pearl
flowers inlayed

on the top

I reflected on
my love for mama
and my happiness
at finding her a pretty gift
but I did not want
to go back and live
with her and daddy
my deep ideals
and trust in them
the meat of my faith in Jesus
had been systematically
butchered
I was left with
the rattling skeleton
of lost ideology

Christmas Day arrived
anticipation seeped
from my pores
Panda and I woke early
quivering with unparalleled
excitement, this magical
kind of Christmas morning
something I had not even
remotely, experienced
both of us poking
sniffing around the little
pile of presents
under the tiny potted tree
tantalizing suspense
finally ended
of course, we sipped
hot spiced tea
while we opened
gifts, purchased with
love, wrapped with care
I felt cherished

and my heart
was full, something
so unexpected
had become a lifeline

Sister Grace and I
had chosen a warm
woolen sweater
for Brother Herb
twisting fall colors
of pumpkin, amber
and warm nutmeg
for Sister Grace
a Russian Cookbook
and a hand painted
silk scarf in greens and
blues, for me a beautiful
lei made of seashells
a ceramic teapot trivet
Sequoia's alphabet
carved into the
circular pattern
and of course
two new books
Russian Fairytales
and Dickens
A Tale of Two Cities

I muffled sobs, and quietly mourned

Carton's selflessness
at end of the book
while I savored
the sense of wonder
and relief, Darnay
was spared, through a
selfless act of love
completely tranced
from the iconic beginning
"It was the best of times. it was the worst of times"
all the way to its
heart rending final lines
"It is a far, far better thing that I do, than I have ever done, it is a far better rest that I go to than I have ever known."

again Brother Herb
initiated discussion
how is it possible
for wisdom and folly
belief and disbelief
light and dark
everything and nothing
to exist in the
same moment?

real truth may lie
in our actions
resurrection and
transformation
are always possible
though great sacrifice
may be required
happiness is not always
sparkling and idealistic
it may rest in the simplicity
of regard for others

in time, Brother Herb
proved this when he made
a great sacrifice for me

Seeds sown so long ago

unwittingly harvested
over many years
crop value sharply intense
in the course of my life
expect duality from
the human element
do not be surprised by
the light and dark
yin and yang
of any person

Herb and Grace
illuminated my darkness
glimmered silently
like a path of moonbeams
over black and dangerous water
did they know
they saved me from
insanity, possibly
dissociative disorder?
I try to remember if
I told them how I felt
but I fear I was already blunted
had become uncomfortable
with spontaneous declarations

while transcribing these memories
I experienced wrenching emotion
long buried under the weight
of life and subsistence
over the course of several days
I found myself weeping
for the things I
cannot go back and say to a
wonderful lumpy lionheart
I made it to his deathbed in 2008
but I missed his last breaths by several minutes

CHAPTER 51 – Russian Dinner Party

Approved by Brother Leo for viewing in theaters

"Fiddler on the Roof"
adults in The Park made
arrangements to go see it
in the last few months
of 1971, well-loved and
talked about, a resultant
Russian themed dinner party
blossomed into reality
decreed by Brother Leo
coordinated by Brother Herb
based on his love
of Russian history
literature and food

Sister Grace prepared
beautiful red borsht
meat pirozhki, tabbouleh
Russian blini with strawberries
and cream, one of the
few times she got really
irritated with me, set me to
help prepare the strawberries
I got carried away with
my adult job and cut off
the whole top of the berry

Brother Herb covered
the kitchen table with an
old cloth, brought in
the ornate Samovars
allowed me to help polish
them to blissful gleaming
beauty, though I was
disappointed to learn

they were made
of brass and not gold
large Manzanita
branches, still adorned
with red berries, gathered
and sprayed snowy white
placed in one Samovar
décor for the center table
the other would be used
to serve hot Russian tea
as the fervor grew
the ideas did as well
soon it turned into a
costume dinner party
adults would now arrive
dressed in Russian themed
clothing and hats

Sister Grace spent hours
at her sewing machine
turning yards of heavy material
golden, red, black, and bronze
glossy striped floral
and geometric designs
into a collared, ribbed
tunic for Brother Herb
and a dress for her

children watched their parents
become Cossacks, with long black
mustachios, great swathes
of fur draped over shoulders
belted tunics over baggy pants
tucked into leather boots
swords at sides, Major Generals
sported gold braid epaulets
Brother Gene had a huge
pair of fur gloves
ladies dressed in fancy gowns

with great bouffant hairdo's
threaded with jewels
regal as the Tsar's court

it was a great success
food was cooked
to perfection, the ladies
practiced and performed
many songs from the
musical score
my brother-in-law dressed
as Rebbe Tevye and
sang, *"If I were a Rich Man"*

for me there was
some recognition
adults were allowed
to do things the
children could not
it is possible I felt this
more acutely than others
still disfellowshipped
from any activities
with the kids

even in my new world
there was some silence
no ideas spoken, or allowed
to come from inside in regard
to injustices in The Park
I kept those thoughts
even from Herb and Grace
we did not discuss
realities, we spoke in
philosophies and possibilities
but like, *Les Misérables*
brewing vexation inside

"We exclaim within ourselves without breaking the external silence. There is a great tumult within; everything within us speaks, except the tongue. The realities of the soul, though not visible and palpable, are nonetheless realities."

voice suppressed, words
moored like a ship in dry dock
sails stowed, waiting

CHAPTER 52 – Spring in Prescott

Spring of 1972, I had been with Herb and Grace

for a year, Brother Leo
had taken ill, seemed
to be out of commission
for some time
that and sharply
decreased interaction
with the other kids
seems I was forgotten
or God stopped speaking to him
in his brown bathroom

in my seclusion
I found freedom
I clung and climbed
like new green ivy
in the sweet bricked sanctuary
I found with Herb and Grace
identified deeply
with passionate
exclamations
from *Les Misérables*

"What a great thing, to be loved! What greater thing still, to love! The heart becomes heroic through passion, if no one loved, the sun would go out."

love I could not
form into words
filled with the sneaking guilt
of abandoning
daddy and mama
the loss of my profound
birth bond and love
for them, before
The Servant of The Lord

showed them my sins
and they cast me out

I contemplated
this mystery, love of
family, the significance
of raising righteous children
made a vow
I dared not voice
but sown regardless
into the space
between subconscious
and consciousness
permanent, indelible
as the Ten Commandments
carved by the almighty
hand of God
into hard Sinai stone

If I have children, I will never turn my face from them. I don't care how sinful they are. We will burn together, because I will go to hell with them before I will let anyone hurt them or take them from me!

Spring is always beautiful in Prescott, perfect climate

for planting a pink trumpet lily
my reward for a good report card

sitting in a little pot, one of the new delights
accumulated for the planting season

carefully watered and monitored
until a fine fresh Saturday morning

it would grow with me and return again
every year taller and stronger, we

wandered through the groundcover
peony bushes, and variegated blooms

looking for the perfect spot to
plant my lily, settled on the corner

near the back patio so it could be supported
by the corner awning pole as it grew

Panda romped in the garden while
we dug our little hole and carefully placed

the sprouted bulb, covered it with mulch
and marked it with a little picture card

this would be my responsibility, watering
weeding, nurturing to vibrant pink beauty

Panda plopped down to sniff curiously
at the neat mound of damp earth, tiny green

sprouts poking through, we settled in the sun
open on my lap *"The Last of The Mohicans"*

content together, his head on my knee
my hand burrowed deep in his scruff

Nearing my 11th birthday,

I had been with
Herb and Grace for
almost eighteen months
we were a family

I continued to walk
to school alone
always an oddity
but my weirdness
had become
somewhat routine
still, any caged freak
is worth poking
occasionally

in The Park
I was generally
left to myself, outside
of backwards movies
and occasional
summons for
a beating just
because I was me
and must be
reminded of
my wicked nature

I learned to
appreciate the
autonomy of
walking, free of
supervision
separate from the
group, lost in
my own world
building the future
in my head

CHAPTER 53 – Awakened Serpent

I caught the end of a quiet conversation between Brother Herb and Sister Grace

I heard her say
"It has been long enough. I am going to talk to him."
quiet consent
from him
no more was said

she bathed and
dressed with great care
put on a light blue suit
with a slim skirt
hooked her purse
on her arm like a shield
and left the house
walking down
the road, a duchess
seeing to her duty
Herb and I enjoyed
breakfast of
red grapes, sliced apples
and hot Earl Grey tea
with lemon

she returned smiling
took a seat on
the couch and
delivered the news
I was no longer
disfellowshipped
restored to regular status
with the other
children, just in time
for my 11th birthday
Esther and I would

Be allowed to have
a birthday party
together, and invite
Becky and Angela

I don't know
what she said to
Brother Leo, but
she did it for me
bearded the
leviathan in his lair
I felt lighter
it was like being
released from prison
with time served

none of us realized
we poked the
dormant serpent
incited him to move into
bait and slither mode
he recognized
devotion and care
deliberately set his
intention to destroy
our deep bond

11th birthday arrived bright and sunny

I chose cheese fondue
which seemed suitable
for eleven-year-old girls
Sister Grace arranged
games for us to play
we blew out eleven candles
on our birthday cake
unrestricted fun
after long deprivation

reconnecting with
Esther was not
what I expected
subdued, she looked
around my sanctuary
saw the trappings
of an only child, slightly
indulged, decorated
to my whims, my visions
my fantasies hanging
on the walls, my books
stacked on the shelves
she had not been so lucky
placed with an older sibling
she slept in a sleeping
bag on the floor
in a room she shared
with their sons

school year 1972
going into 6th grade
was so much better
my hair had grown
enough to be
almost normal

and I could walk
with the other kids
no longer the outsider

I was placed in charge of younger

girls, given responsibility
teach them how to scrub the
floors, in grids of four
floor tiles at a time
demonstrated floor
waxing technique
careful not to put
prints on drying wax

life with Herb and Grace
continued along
but I began to hear
similar whisperings
just like I used to hear
from mama, especially
after a summons
"Why, what did she do?"

back in the collective
punishments resumed
increased in intensity
usually after being
seen by Brother Leo, I
walked reluctantly to The Office
plagued with helplessness
and the familiar stomach ache
when a summons came

I sought comfort
from Panda, eagerly
willing to snuggle
curled around him
heart beats mingled
calm achieved through
unconditional canine
acceptance, Herb and Grace

consoled me with the
most effective gifts
time and books

Brother Leo's secretary arrives with a summons

I follow her rapid
no nonsense strides
to The Office, I am
ordered to sit on the floor
and wait without speaking
leaving, she closes the
door behind her

an older teenage girl
well known to me
is already there
sitting nervously
on a dark gold
cloth covered chair
skirt pulled neatly
over her knees
she is silent as well
anxiety registered
in the hot red flush
across her cheeks

sitting in the corner
on the floor, a little
boy, also well known to me
golden curls escape
from the shitty
underwear he is
wearing on his head
waistband across
his nose, peeping
from the leg holes
long lashed puppy
brown eyes
speaking shame
"don't look at me"

I totally understand
my heart hurts for him
painfully aware
I can't help him
she can't help him
she can't help me
all of us will suffer today

waiting silently
my eyes settle on a
fancy little banzai tree
made of carved stone blossoms
pink rose quartz, purple amethyst
leaves of light and dark green jade
beautiful, exotic focal point
displayed on a half round table
against the wall, revolting
something to hate as much
as I hate The Office
directed to clean
the thing just last week
with hot water
Q-tips and Flaxoap
dreaded chore, hosted fizzing
anxiety, much too close
to Brother Leo's abode
likely he laid eyes on me
thus, the summons

Brother Will, handsome
nemesis arrives, starts
with teenage companion
indicates she should
get on her knees
in front of the chair
she does this self consciously
smoothing her skirt down
over sweet, newly
rounded hips and thighs

every time he lashes
her, the leather wallop
flips her skirt up

morbidly, I watch
the flesh on the back
of her thighs wobble
under the force of the blows
reddened weals gather
and begin to overlap
hot pink and angry
on her pale skin
I catch a glimpse of
her modest white panties
embroidered with pink
flowers, Brother Will
notices too, chuckling
he deliberately
strikes to achieve
the same effect
over and over again
enjoying his job
echoes of Edmond Dantes
billow like a black omen

"He doomed these men to every known torment his inflamed imagination could devise, while still considering that the most frightful were too mild, and above all, too brief for them."

I lower my eyes
hiding bitterness
impotent rage
helplessness, feel
molten flames redden
my own face, I can
change nothing today

"For all evils there are two remedies, time and silence"

I feel fierce
internal tension
like a coiling snake
looking to spring
someday

I endure my beating
the familiar acid fire
of leather lashes
battering, bruising
can't stop tears
hold onto a hot a
thready mirage, an
idea, I would be
equal in resolve to
Edmond Dantes
could not reconcile
forgiveness like
Jean Valjean

my beating, not
entertaining as that of
a prettily rounded teen girl
concludes with
efficient brutality
he allows me to
scurry out of The Office
I left the little boy
in fecal shame, hoping
shitty underwear
turbaned round his
head would be
punishment enough

back in my sanctuary
curled up with a book
"The Hunchback of Notre Dame"
shame and seared nerve
endings soothed

with restorative words

"His cathedral was enough for him. It was peopled with marble figures of kings, saints, and bishops who at least did not laugh in his face and looked at him only with tranquility and benevolence."

my books would need
to be enough for now

CHAPTER 54 – Sanctified Poachers

I am not sure when the poaching started but I was always aware of it

all the girls my age knew
Esther, Angela, Becky and I
designated to babysit
a group of the younger kids
on the weekends during
hunting season, a familiar
event in The Park
we were used to seeing
dead game animals
brought to the large trees
by The Dining Hall and Big Patio
hung, bled, and skinned
there were many tags
but it hardly mattered
we poached what we wanted
or thought we needed

annoyed when I heard it was meant
to be a secret, forced to pretend I had no idea
as the children were not to know of
these illicit deeds, the women spent
long days butchering deer and elk
cutting, grinding hamburger
packaging steaks and rump roasts
stew meat was canned
for storage in the root cellars

conscripted to babysit in one
of the double wide trailers
with its own washer and dryer
the four of us arrived early
each morning, charged with
the care of five to seven children
babies in diapers and

potty trained toddlers
diapers for each baby
marked on the edge
with different colored
nail polish, wouldn't
wash away, but I had
questions in my mind
why the women would
have colored nail polish
available to mark diapers
my curiosity was singular
none of the other girls
seemed to care

we were given explicit
instructions for diaper changes
fingers under the fold so we
wouldn't accidentally pin the baby
rubber pants pulled over that
"We do not want to see any diaper rashes"
rinsed in diaper pails with
hot water and bleach before
going in the washer
diapers were washed, dried
and folded neatly into stacks

food and bottles were laid out
expectation that all would
be done *exactly* as directed
babies bathed and sweet smelling
when their mothers picked
them up, end of the day

we had raucous fun watching
Becky feed one of the babies mashed
green peas, some went in his mouth
and the rest all over his face and into
his hair, sweet dimpled smile
one tooth gleaming from a green

goblin mask, burbling baby giggles
as she airplaned food into
his adorable little chops

one young mother arrived
to find her infant with a diaper rash
we had not changed him correctly
directed us into the
master bedroom for a lesson
on proper diaper changing
demonstrated careful cleansing
of tiny penis and walnut scrotum
sternly lectured, while
fanning her hand across
clean genitals to dry them
she turned back to her infant
still speaking when an arching spout
of baby pee, shot up into
her face and open mouth

spluttering, she grabbed
a clean diaper, clapped it over
baby boy parts, now soiled again
her sweet baby reached for his toes
grasping with chubby little fingers
unconcerned by the fuss his
mama made, spitting
and rubbing her mouth

trying hard not to laugh
we gaped, slyly enjoying
a tiny degree of payback
she sighed; red faced
and surprisingly, she
began to chuckle, it
was not so long ago
she was a kid in The Park
suffered under the lash
for miniscule infractions

she decided in that
moment, not to step
into the black abyss
have us physically chastised
released from fear
we all laughed together

A couple of old school buses

helped with the deception
likely because they did not want
kids inadvertently spilling
the beans at school
local Game Wardens were onto us
but never caught us red handed

over in The Garage, daddy
the resident mechanic, rebuilt an
old blue Dodge car, welded a metal
panel on the bottom, used it to bump
through the woods at night
 "Shining for elk"
animals were quartered and hauled
home in large galvanized tubs, snuck
into The Toddle House in the
wee hours, to be prepped
and packaged the next day

meals at The Toddle House
suspended for a time
diversion and food provided
on the buses, stripped and rebuilt
seats turned to face each other
with a table in the middle
like rolling yellow diners
they bussed us around to
Jerome, the old ghost town
the *Petrified Forest*
Bedrock City, and the
Grand Canyon Caverns

it seems, to be nabbed
while poaching was
a much bigger concern
than other events
in The Park, including

extreme whipping sessions
and battered children

these trips were some of
the most enjoyable
of my life in The Park
arranged as cover
for illicit actions
bumping down the road
in those old buses
we sang freely, raucously
my sister-in-law knew
every song in the world

"Zoom de ada, zoom de ada, zoom de ada, zo-ooom. I love the mountains, I love the rolling hills, I love the daffodils, I love the fireside when all the lights are low, zoom de ada, zoom de ada!"

I wanted with burning intensity
to up-stage her, singing

"There's a hole in the bottom of the sea. There's a hole.... there's a hole.... there's a hole in the bottom of the sea. There's a germ on the spot, on the wing, on the flea, on the hair, on the wart, on the frog, on the knot, on the log, in the hole, in the bottom of the sea!"

I practiced relentlessly
in the woods by the creek
ready for the next trip
and a chance to take
a deep breath and keep up
with her, singing faster and faster
real satisfaction on the
unusual day I pulled that off

these were the times
when I wondered if the adults
might enjoy a different
connection with
the children, one of

communication
fun, enlivened education
but they always returned
to the grim overlord
took instruction
ignored internal unrest

CHAPTER 55 – A New Family Arrives in The Park

I had one more wonderful Christmas with Herb and Grace

gifted with a set of vinyl records
American Indian drumming and chanting
"Ho ka heh wa nah, no weh"
no idea what the words
meant, loved them anyway
the sound of those drums vibrated
in the soles of my feet
filled my stomach, expanded
my ribcage, filled my ears
spoke to me of primal rhythm

I wanted to abandon
Godly instruction, expectations
thump my feet into the ground
raise brown dust puffs
circle, circle, circle, fly… fly… fly…
never acted on that wild desire
stuck on an enforced religious
and very strict path for girls

come spring, my lily
bloomed, tall and regal
long delicate pink trumpets
with deep magenta throats
sporting bright yellow stamen
the most beautiful
flowers I'd ever seen

I finished the 6th grade
and was nearing my twelfth
birthday when a new
and exciting family
came to visit in The Park
sound of my fluted

recorder woke me from sleep

a boy I had never seen
sat in the chair by my door
playing piping notes, didn't
sound any better than mine
white blonde hair, longer
than Park standards
faded tee-shirt, rock band logo
on the front, would never
be allowed in The Park
cautiously, I sat up

"Hi, I'm Bruce"

from Canada, acquaintances
of Herb and Grace
a dozen people traveling
in an old aqua blue van
his parents, their five kids
and five Cree Nation kids
they were fostering

Brother Leo arranged
a grand welcome for them
special events and meetings
kids in The Park
youngest to oldest
rounded up, given instruction
painstakingly coached
through the score of
"The Sound of Music"
all the way from
"The Hills are alive......" to
"So long farewell, I hate to say goodbye......."
directed by my sister-in-law
presented, a brilliant
success, at The Dining Hall

another large family
overwhelmed
by gracious and
loving Christianity
needed a life in The Park
started the lengthy
immigration process
and left Canada behind
moved to The Park
minus the Cree Nation kids
brought with them
enlightened enthusiasm
and fresh blood

Bruce became a
childhood companion
and a lifelong friend
along with his siblings
eventually, our families
had another connection
when my brother
married his sister

CHAPTER 56 – Brother Herb saves Panda

I believed I would be with

Herb and Grace forever
they were everything to me

didn't realize the draconian reptile
was always watching, his plan

had not worked the way he
intended, I was not an affliction

uncultured troublesome child, foisted on
an educated, formal couple, rather

we become an entity, enmeshed
affectionate, flawed perfection

father, mother, child and dog
connective biology unimportant

I don't know why he needed
to tear us apart, wasn't sure

what he hated in me, why
he felt the need to smite me

he had mama where he
wanted her, broken and numb

always dozing on her couch
uncaring, not remembering

events of the day, when she
was awake, it was to do her stint

at The Dining Hall, daddy was

gone all the time, away and

out of sight, trucking huge
loads of drywall all over

the state to current and
future construction sites

we were out in the garden
when the Brothers came for Panda

by now, I knew what was
coming when the henchmen

showed up with questions
about the family pet

Panda had been seen nosing
around in someone else's yard

sent by *The Servant of The Lord*
they were there to kill him

ever present .22 tucked in a waistband
warm summer sun disappeared

in smoke and ash, how had I let
myself believe in happily ever after?

grief streaked across my heart
like a cold wet finger on sooty glass

this would happen just like before
Panda would be a lifeless pile

of meat and fur, snuffed of light
and anime, soured imagination went

all the way to digging his grave

in our garden, wooden cross

barren of a savior, standing
over him like a broken promise

on my knees in the damp earth, I
clutched at Panda's collar *"No...no...no..."*

Brother Herb stooped toward me
softly, calmly, hand on my head

"Deborah, let me have him"

I looked up into his calm, steady
eyes as he reached down and

picked Panda up in his arms
pulled him tight against his chest

turned to the doggie executioners
"Ok, go ahead and shoot"

what was happening? this
couldn't be real, astonishment

edged through panic, a brilliant
slash of light through a cracked door

very steady, holding Panda
close, he stepped toward them

"This child loves the dog and she doesn't deserve this, but if you are compelled to shoot, go ahead. I won't stop you."

his eyes bulged a little
behind his glasses

but he held their gaze
and stood firm, Panda

picked up on the tension
in his arms and body

whined, licked his chin
I couldn't breathe

they were speaking but
I could not hear a word

the only sound in my head
static buzzing, dimmed reality

I watched them walk away
and Brother Herb gently

placed Panda back in my arms
I clutched him and breathed

wet faced, into his scruff, he whined
twisted, frantically licked my cheek

through the shock, dawning
perception, Brother Herb stood

in defense of me, and my dog
my own parents did not do that

quietly, with resolve, he
determined right and wrong

rebuffed directives delivered from
The Servant of the Lord to a follower

he must have known there would
be a sacrifice but he recognized

the damage to my psyche and soul
might be irreparable, Panda

was spared, but my fairytale
life with Herb and Grace

came to a crashing end

CHAPTER 57 – The Serpent Strikes

Hooded cobra gave us just enough time to think we escaped his venom

before he summoned
Brother Herb, I would be
moved to my sister's house
just one door over

our beautiful garden backed
up to her trailer, nothing else in
years of rebuke and menticide
crushed me so completely as

this news, delivered just before
I was sent to babysit one of
my nephews for the evening
everything would change

my chest felt ripped apart by the
burgeoning tombstone of grief
beneath my ribs, I put my nephew to bed
and curled up in a ball, let meteoric

sorrow carry me to the limits
of impotent despair, surely this
torment was great as Samson's
when he stood between two

pillars and tore a building down
upon his own head, if only I could do
the same, trepidation wormed in
my belly, as I gave rein to lucid visons

Brother Leo smashed flat as a stink bug
beneath a ton of stones, nothing left
of him but bilious ooze, could I welcome
death to annihilate this serpent?

weary melancholy followed those
imaginings, I was no Samson, no David
no agent of God, to destroy the Philistine
defeated, heartsick, I gave up, cried like I

have never cried before or after that day
like a broken dam, hot tears flooded down
my face, dripped off my chin and soaked
my collar, drowned any tiny ember of hope

Brother Leo, the coiling serpent in my garden
would *never* stop until my heart was nothing
more than shredded red meat, butchered
hanging from the lintel of my soul like a

swinging carcass, a vast bloody curtain to
stain everything passing through with
moral anguish. bitter pain, and burning
irredeemable hate, like Dantes, I understood

"The heart breaks when it has swelled too much in the warm breath of hope, then finds itself enclosed in cold reality."

my brother and his wife did not seem
to notice my tear streaked, swollen face
they chastised me for leaving dirty
dishes in the sink, the ones they

used and left before I got there
they couldn't hurt me more
with a scarcely noted rebuke
later, I crept into my sanctuary

knowing it would be gone tomorrow
my childhood shriveled up, became
a desiccated wad of perished dreams
I garrisoned that death with resolve

I would never let him or anyone else
hurt me like this again, exhausted body
gave up, numbed senses took over
dragged me into twitching slumber

distantly, through black desolation
I heard Sister Grace sobbing, another
helpless woman, as heartbroken as I
woke the next day forever changed

just before my 12th birthday, any
childish vulnerability successfully
barricaded in my brick stronghold
quietly, Sister Grace helped me pack

unspoken regret and sorrow heavy in
the air, I left carrying so much more than
I arrived with, my eyes puffy and reddened
but dry, I patted Panda on the head

resisted a snuggle, promised to
come see him, knew I would not
craggy abyss stretched from head to
heart, deep, dark, and permanent

she walked me to my sister's
house, less than 50 yards away
put a million miles between us
my sister, a married adult with

a child before I was born, didn't
seem much like a sibling, I hoped
it would not be too horrible
I couldn't know she had already

been directed by Brother Leo
to *"set on"* me, keep me *"in line"*
scrutinize every move, report back
to him any minutiae, intimate details

from my new bedroom window
I could see Panda, my beautiful lily, and
my former life, glimpsed Herb and Grace
on many days, taking tea on their patio

the next two years turned me to oak

I understood the change
knew I was not a better person
for it, worked to hide the
injury and resultant fury

borrowed from *The Count*
reasons for internal conflict
needed to right a terrible wrong
a child, without power, I could not

"Moral wounds have this peculiarity, they may be hidden, but they never close, always painful, ready to bleed when touched, they remain fresh and open in the heart."

I lived on and I learned to hide
fiery thoughts, I would roil and
brood, then silently decide what
I felt, and assign a Biblical absolute

"Just like a tree that's planted by the water, I…. shall… not…. be…. moved!"

CHAPTER 58 – No Longer a Child

Age of accountability arrived for me

with demented punctuality
life with my oldest sister
immediately awful
no nonsense, tight lipped

insistent upon cleanliness
grating trouble for
leaving hair in the bathroom
sink, sure to find anything

missed with the dust cloth
or vacuum cleaner, never
leave a dish in the sink
or eat without permission

most excruciating, required
to load up my only friends
my books, classics, watch them
burn, in smoldering wisps, hid

my fury as pages caught, burst
into orange flames, danced to ash
Ivanhoe's face flickered, blackened to
char, vanished in smokey plumes

that fire consumed my joy, I would be
allowed to read the Bible and listen
to tapes, but no outside books, no time
for indulgent reading, art, or creativity

it was time for me to knuckle down
learn responsibility and the work
of the women, anything else
was wasted effort and time

My twelfth birthday came and went

an uncelebrated milestone, important only
in terms of accountability and an adult future
I shared a room with my four-year-old niece

family dynamic, dysfunctional at best
my sister, a victim to religion, sold
her life down the river of decisions made

by daddy and *The Servant of The Lord*
she left her first husband, the Navy man
signed over parental rights to her two

oldest sons, married a man chosen for her
had no desire to be married but he was also
snared in a trap of religious expectations

an attempt to fix his homosexuality
using marriage to an eligible divorcee
with knowledge of the nuptial bed

short, stout as an ox, quick witted, with
a sweet, infectious smile, a hard worker
journeyman drywall hanger and mudder

under duress, beaten badly, he was thrown
into her bed to consummate their union
they had 3 children, one died at birth, and

their life became a succession of screaming
fights, followed by dismal silences and
strained ignoring of each other, I noted

the bottle of *Boones Farm* in the fridge
wine in a religious house, where it is
strictly forbidden, bitterly confused

by the lack of moral standards

I was held to with an iron rod, life
worsened as it seemed like my sister

took Brother Leo's directives seriously
yard dog mean, I could not do anything right
I became a convenient outlet for her frustrations

nights were spent in twisted misery, difficult
sleep, haunting nightmares, waking shaking and
sweaty, hands on my head, clutching my hair

coming into puberty, my body changing daily
noted sharp oniony body odor, scattered
pimples on my skin, coarse dark hairs on my legs

taken to task for being smelly, wearing
underwear for too long, she took to inspecting
my panties before they went into the wash

this humiliation coupled with complaints of using
too much toilet paper, wasting it, or failing to
use enough, completed my loss of control over

secret bodily functions, provoked gloaming
anger, required to start putting my hair up in curlers
difficult, as I still avoided mirrors, forced to pull on

panty hose and then an old-fashioned girdle of
tight rayon and cotton, over that a rayon slip
covered it all with long skirts and dresses

I was smothered in layers of modest clothing
swaddled discomfort, sweaty thighs and
nether regions the price for being a female

but the worst humiliation was that leg hair
long and dark, sticking through or mashed flat
under nude nylon stockings, I endured constant

harassment and stinging insults from other kids
my sister refused to let me shave my legs, even
worse, purchased old lady patent leather loafers

those horrible, horrible shoes were the thing
I could not endure. I cried silently and bitterly
I could see no way to avoid wearing them

miraculously, before I was required to wear them
to school, they disappeared off the matt at the
door, vanished, possibly my brother-in-law

saved me, still, my sister believes I threw them in
the garbage, as if I would have risked the reprisal
in pain, following a brazen action like that

testament to astounding ignorance and lack of
awareness many of the adults demonstrated in regard
to actual fear generated in the children of The Park

they assumed we are wind up Christians
happy to suffer the lash for the sake of our souls
perhaps this was the delusion that allowed

The Park to continue as long as it did

My older sister

now a befuddled, elderly lady
sweet, kind, self-deprecatory
a fragile grey bird, flying into windows
moves through life, forever stunned
she asked and I have offered
unreserved forgiveness
for my horrible life
in her house
no hint of the woman
I lived with all those
years ago

she will say
"I guess I was pretty awful"
I don't think she
understands the degree of
personal invasion I suffered
because she was unable to assign
individual rights to a child
simply progeny, to do the will
of parents, religious leaders
and God, she never
assigned any rights to herself
an unworthy woman

she said she did
what she was told to do
she had no rebellion in her
overcome with fear for her soul
and aversion to tribulation
a simple pawn, frustrated in a
marriage designed by others
no element of control
over her own life
in her way as miserable as I

*I started my first year of Junior High, 7*th *grade*

excited to have my own locker, carry a
bag lunch, walk to school with a smaller

group of kids, unescorted by Park Sisters
the library was much bigger, an exciting

prospect, weekends labor intensive
for girls our age, old enough to

start cooking, early to The Dining Hall
we stood in front of a bank of hots stoves

fried bacon and eggs for hours
sometimes, sausage and pancakes

buttered endless piles of toast, shucked
mountainous buckets of shrimp for a special

meal, seemed like hundreds of tablecloths
must be washed and bleached, often

I had a wash basket full of long white
tablecloths to iron perfectly, no missed

corners or ironed in wrinkles, that would
mean a do over of the whole basket before

school on Monday morning, I found time
to read hidden books, under my covers with

stolen flashlight, blunted outer world calm
found in written thoughts and expressions

I gave my mind free range during tedious
time consuming work, fantasized about a

different life, wondered what I would be doing

differently if I were a rich and powerful magus

able to change lives with a thought or wave of
my hand, I yearned for magical abilities

while resigned to the practical impossibility
indulged in secretly guarded supply of

biographies, myths, and total fiction, my new
favorite, *"Mara, Daughter of the Nile"*

a stubborn slave, her master, afraid
of her blue eyes, beat her frequently

an unusual female, she did not bend or
bow, she became a rebel, led a revolution

and gained for herself a better life and *freedom*
this fairytale, embodied my desire to be a

female who forces change, still dismally sure
I had no future other than an arranged

marriage, life of slavery to a man and religion
adept at sneaking books home, I didn't have

a book bag, held them in my arms and draped
my sweater or coat over them, sidled into the

house, stashed them between mattress
and box springs, opened the door one day to

my enraged sister, I had not even stepped
over the threshold when she smashed a

broom over my head, broke it in half
my vision winkled and I dropped the stack

of sweater wrapped books, clutched my head

angry tears stinging my eyes, what was that for?

I left a layer of dust on the top of the refrigerator
when I was directed to clean the house

mop and wax the floors, vacuum
all of the rooms, scrub the bathrooms

and toilets, carefully dust the multitude
of fancy car shaped Avon bottles lined up

on shelves beside the door, I envisioned
carrying glass cars to the woods, shrieking

heaving, smashing them against the granite
boulders until they were nothing but a pile

of multicolored silica dust, I moored that
venom with heavy rope and hard control

now doubly bad, my books spilled out into
the floor, she demanded to know where I was

keeping them, clever hiding place discovered
at least she let me take them back to school

I began reading books during class, hiding them
within my text books, appeared to be studious, but

lost in fantasy, uncaring of Social Studies, English
and Math, my grades started to drop but nobody

cared, least of all my sister, school was
unimportant for girls in our age group

the knot on my head went down over the
next few weeks, but I was cautious around

my sister for much longer, she was distraught

with her life and her marriage, but I only saw

the angry side, it seems life in The Park was
devastating for many people, there was no

happiness in her home, she lived every
day with disappointment and a feeling

of failure, bound by religion to be the
obedient wife and mother, betrayed by

emotion, humiliation, and sexual frustration
she had a dangerous overdose of Valium

often her children and I hid in the back bedroom
while she raged at her husband, and threw things

once, toothpicks, hundreds of them strewn
from kitchen to front room, he would remain silent

cause for greater frustration and impotent anger
mired in an emotional wasteland, we lived without

sweet peace and Christian charity, no *Holy Ghost*
to be found within those close paneled walls

So, it became the Bible for me, no more fairytales and fiction

I read with total attention because
it's all I had, well versed in the creation
story, Noah and the Ark, Moses and the
Ten Commandments, the parting of the Red Sea

cached many stories not read before
conflict between Moses and his sister Miriam
adored the story of Esther and Mordechai
sympathized with Orpah, Ruth, and Naomi

grinned like a loon, reading about lovely Tamar
widowed twice, with child by whoredom, slyly
outwitted Judah, she, more righteous than he
produced his signet and staff, proved paternity

admired the cunning Jael, lured Sisera with
food and sleep, hammered a tent peg through
his temple, pinned his head to the ground
embraced God's grace for Rahab the harlot

reveled in the wisdom and strength of Deborah
advisor to the great General Barak, longed to
emulate this biblical female judge and mediator
who held righteous, confident dominion over men

struggled through religious laws and rules
of the Old Testament, stumped by awful
terror texts, rejected outright the horrible
parable of a lowly woman, sent to her death

by the men of her house, raped and abused
to spare her husband from the sexual
intentions of the wicked *"Sons of Belial"*
worthy sacrifice of an unworthy woman

died with her hands on the threshold
of her door, so her husband could hack her

body into twelve pieces, rotting sections
sent, urgent message to the tribes of Israel

used as bloody currency to purchase
righteous fervor, raise the wrath of war
I internalized these ancient segments
but could not comprehend the lesson

Abraham's sacrifice, profoundly
understood, metaphorically suffered that
fate, but I had no faith, had not seen God
speak from the heavens to save me

no ram caught in the bushes
to spare me, moment of the knife
God stood on high, always distant
obedience his demand, stripes

for his suffering, taken from my hide
my humiliation, for his humiliation
unlike him, I did not grow in love
and compassion, I became hard inside

ultimately unsatisfied with biblical fare
I needed more, set my mind to find it
I wanted now stories, now people
now conflicts, and current resolutions

Esther and I continued to exist like pawns on Brother Leo's chessboard

the weakest of his players, easily sacrificed
Esther had also been moved to another home
always nail biting, jittery, nervous, and unhappy

disgusted by wet slobbery kisses, uncomfortable
touching, from the man of the house, avoided him

when she could, frequently vulnerable at night, unsure
of dream versus fact, we talked about mama and daddy while
doing chores, wondered if we would ever go back home

there was always extra work for girls our age
we met at The Toddle House to make sandwiches

on Saturday and Sunday afternoons, carried large tubs
pulled along red wagons, went house to house, passing
food in place of an official meal at The Toddle House

I hated living with our sister, just wanted to be free
but we were stalled in the world of The Park while

Brother Leo and the adults whittled away at our tomorrows
our sins and chastisements publicly visible, their vices,
allowances and sins, hidden from sight, we understood

there was no future for us other than the one dictated by
this cult and our family, hanging on the words of a dead prophet

now disenchanted with the life they dragged us to
whether they realized it or not, safely blinded by
chosen allegiance and cognitive dissonance

CHAPTER 59 – Jezebel Masquerade

It was just a dab of purple eye shadow

Sharon borrowed it
from a friend
swiped it on her
eyelids at school
carefully rubbed
it off before
going home, but
she missed a bit
her sin discovered
by our sister-in law

she paid for that
in pain, after her
beating, our brother
threw all of her
clothes out into
the lawn, bodily
picked her up
and threw her
out the door
to land in the grass
the mattress
from her bed
flew out, plopped
on top of her
dresser drawers
followed
a miserable day
spent, cleaning
up her things
lesson ingrained
with dolorous
biblical wrath

"Did you ever notice the first woman ever used makeup on her face, Jezebel, what happened to her and you know what God did to her, he fed her to the dogs. So, you see, that's dog meat, all right, just so, just the palms of her hands and her skull left."

Work continued to pour in, bids for huge drywall jobs were accepted

all over the state
almost all involved
HUD housing projects
boys left school
after 8th grade to
become drywallers
hangers and mudders
soon became apparent
the men would need
to stay on the jobs
return home on
the weekends
to get as much done
in the work week
as possible
arrangements were
made for two of the
women or two teenage
girls to go along
each week to plan
and prepare meals
wash piles of laundry

Brother Leo reaped
the rewards of
this added income
bought a new Cadillac
though, he didn't seem to
leave his home as much
he looked worse
every time I saw him
sick, puffy, and pale
obsidian eyes, clouded
but always looking for
infractions, disobedience
dictating lists to his secretary
punishments for

kids who happened
to catch his attention

I perfected hiding from him
stayed unobtrusive
as possible while working
in The Dining Hall
when he was there
sitting in his large chair
receiving choice bits
of the prepared meal
served with deferential
submission by the Sisters
he continued his strange
penchant for floral cologne
and soft moccasin slippers

a sneaky listener
I heard conversations
not intended for
my ears, adults
believed erroneously
children are docile
completely controlled
without imagination
to put their words
together and
understand what
they are really saying

I heard doubts quietly expressed
whisperings about *"whiskey"*
medications, *"drugs"*
one of the younger women
had been instructed by
The Park nurse in the
technique for giving
The Servant of The Lord
intramuscular injections

of Morphine and Demerol

the area on his hip
so hard from repeated
injections, she broke the needle
suffered the terror of her deed
and waited for consequence
he never noticed, the
efficient Park nurse
directed her to his thigh
my immediate
unvoiced concern
He didn't have his pants on?

I began to understand
all was not right with
our Godly leader but I didn't
understand opiate addiction
my mind burned with resentment
learning that he drank
expensive whiskey

on a regular basis
children of The Park
were humiliated, beaten
and scarred in the name
of obedience to our sect
while *The Servant of The Lord*
broke the commandments
of the Prophet

he began to have private
viewings of movies
and it's possible he
was entertained, even high
in an opiate haze when
he birthed the idea
of a big party, specifically, a
masquerade party

to entertain the women
while the men were out of town
working big drywall jobs

The children watched with jaw dropping

surprise, while the women of The Park
prepared for the masquerade party

a great sense of lighthearted fun enveloped
everyone, planning the meal, choosing characters

Simplicity and *Butterick* costume patterns
everywhere, women busy at sewing machines

delightful materials appeared, sequins, fake fur
sparkling glitter, fringes, wigs, and even *makeup!*

all of us heard the Prophet scream about this sin
"The only woman ever put makeup on her face, Jezebel, and she was eaten by dogs!"

daddy's vicious words echoed in my head
"If I ever see you painted up that way, I'll sever yer head!"

two of the pregnant ladies, dressed full out, as
Tweedle Dee and Tweedle Dum, wearing *pants!*

again, words drilled into memory, resurfaced
"I'll tell you sisters, it's an abomination for a woman to put on clothing that pertains to a man."

unbelievably, *my mama* dressed up like a geisha
eyes painted exotically; hair sprayed coal black

several of them did a *"Jungle Book"* theme
and merrily sang, *"The Bare Necessities"*

there were Indians, and Cowboys, the Godfather
Cleopatra, a Spanish dancer, an Arabian princess,

Sister Edra, dressed in sparkling fringe and sequins
a 20s flapper, sang and *danced* the Charleston

the kids were not invited to this fun event, but we
heard all about it and lots of pictures were taken

this caused a whomping rift in my consciousness
so hard for me to understand, how all of this

could be ok, this was sin for adults surely
as it was sin for the kids, Sharon had been harshly

punished, humiliated for wearing a tiny dab
of purple eye makeup, we carried notes to school

requiring we be removed from square dance
class because dancing was against our religion

I didn't understand the way my own brain
had been bent, my sense of injustice was kindled

I couldn't see past that to recognize a good time
greatly enjoyed by women, in their own way

subverted and controlled much like us, they
were fortunate, no punishment for them

but I was unwilling to concede all of this was
ok for them simply because Brother Leo said so

CHAPTER 60- Bad Timing

Late Summer 1973, I was told to get ready for

my first out of town
assignment
paired with an older
teen girl, going to
Casa Grande for a week
very near the
Gila River Reservation
the Brothers working another
HUD housing project

supplies were stocked
in the small travel
trailer, stationed in
an RV Park near the job
menus written, breakfast
lunch, and dinner for
hungry hard working
men, returned to the
tiny trailer covered
in drywall dust
clothes rinsed out
with the hose, then
into the laundry bucket
lost count of the
tee shirts and jeans
we washed and folded

the trailer outfitted
with rows of bunks
geekily unattractive
I slept unmolested
unusually free from criticism
and rebuke, hard working
tired men snored, farted

and slept, rising at dawn
for coffee and breakfast

we two looked longingly
at the pool, forbidden
to wear swimsuits
intransigent doctrine

"Hmmm Brothers, this might make you want to vomit. strip one of these little women off, stretch them out on a beach somewhere with a bathing suit on, she'll send more men to hell than all the bootleg joints in your city. She makes men fall. The devil knowed that from the beginning."

sparkling aqua blue temptation
irresistible, we opted
to jump in wearing cotton
blouses and skirts
only ones in the pool
in the hours between
lunch and dinner
we enjoyed chlorinated
cannonballs, bellyflops
backflips, and underwater
swimming one end to the other
wet clothes, clean
dried and folded
before the Brothers
returned to the trailer

third day, strange
cramping, throbbing
inferno deep in my pelvis
I woke to first flow
of menstrual blood
staining thighs and sheets
worst possible time
and place for this curse
thankful for the
presence of the older

wiser girl, we folded
thick uncomfortable
squares of paper towel
to make temporary
sanitary napkins

Soon as we got back, I snuck over the rocks to mama

woke her from her
usual position, lying
on her side on the couch
whispered to her
I started my period
she walked back with
me to tell my sister
and life got worse
new and challenging rules
mark the calendar
first and last day of
every cycle
manage sanitary
napkins with
psychotic cleanliness
womanhood now
proclaimed, this rite
of passage
a deranged thing
in my sister's house

loss of privacy
depressingly complete
invasive inspection
of sanitary napkins
stretched all credulity
nasty and unclean
if I didn't change them
often enough
wasteful if I used too many

obsessions to rule
my life, tampons not allowed
for reasons involving
preservation of virginity
a thing required for
marriage to a Godly man

"If a man finds that his wife has known another man before him, he has a biblical right to put her away."

Life moved on, eventually I received a summons from my oldest brother

to appear at an
appointed time and place
fear soured my belly
Esther, Angela
and Becky already
there, waiting but
it wasn't for punishment

escorted into a
meeting in the living room
my brother solemnly
informed us, at age
of accountability
things would be
divulged to us
we would be
expected to act
in adult fashion
preserve secrets
above all, help
with daily work

we were told God
gave us license
to poach the number
of elk and deer
we may need to
sustain life for a large
group of people
this was illegal
but God governed
our actions, so we need
not fear discovery
or prosecution
sharing sly glances
we acted with appropriate
solemnity, and agreed

to preserve the secret

this new feeling of
shared responsibility
for illicit activity
put us on par with
the adults, in some
way changed us
we were no longer
just children to
be coerced along the
straight and narrow
way, we became
participants upholding
the way of The Park

tagged animals
were hung in the trees
at The Dining Hall
and the Big Patio
good show for anyone
with questions
while untagged animals
continued to come
in at night, we
were now part
of the working crew

This is nothing new, a huge elk hangs from the branches of

a large evergreen
blood, coppery
visceral, and thick
in my nostrils
I wield the skinning
knife, along with the
women, as expected

instructed in the
way of cutting rough
winter coat away
from muscle fascia
for a moment
I am still and silent
looking into open
eyes, cloudy death
under a swoop of
soft hairy eyelashes

I feel the need
to speak, apologize
free the beast from
the merciless necessity
that brings him to
our knives
disturbed
by a vision of his
widely open eyes
covered over
with dirt and rocks
when we have finished
stripping his bones
I blink, reactively
reaching to touch a
cold sightless eyeball
push at rubbery
eyelids, I cannot

close them

my inner eye turns
him right side up
sees him find
strength in massive
hindquarters, spring
away with regal intent
look back over his
shoulder, antlers
silhouetted in
the dying sun
leaping through
brush and trees
always away from
the streaking bullets

briefly, Rosie and
her babies flicker in
my memory, painful hot scald
burns behind my lids
throat tightens
sympathy throbs in me
I must, I will....
disconnect...

reach down into
the cold wadded place
inside, reckon logically
our food arrives on
hoof and wing
reject the tide of
feelings generated by
the death of this creature
caught, slaughtered
in the clean green
of his sanctuary
my imaginings
won't keep him

from the stew pots
and canning jars, but
diligent work may keep
me from the lash

CHAPTER 61 – Prayer for the Serpent

Brother Leo is ill, "possibly dying," all are called to prayer, children to

The Chapel, the adults who did not accompany
him to the hospital, met in The Dining Hall
disbelief hung like a pall of oily smoke over The Park
I had seen this before, when the Prophet died, we
children clustered on our knees before the stone altar

Sisters directed us to pray, I was given charge of a group
of younger children to pray with, to beg God, please
spare our servant, Brother Leo, we need his guidance
how will we make the rapture without his leadership?
"Oh, Heavenly Father what will we do?" We cannot lose our shepherd!"

we were never told what was wrong with him, but I
gave ear to the hysterical crying and desperate prayers
the fear and panic went straight to my core, adults of
The Park could not function independently, walk away
from control, they *needed* to be steered, *needed* to be

told, how to earn God's greatest gift, eternal life
I had wished for his death, craved it, imagined it
in technicolor, how could I pray he would live?
my mind wandered, what exactly would happen
if he died, who would take over in his place?

like a nervous cat's tail, invasive thoughts twitched and
whipped, I had never known a different life, we had always
been here, he had always been our shepherd, I found
I was much more curious about what life would be
like if he died than I was fearful for our future

Brother Leo survived his mysterious affliction
returned to The Park with new resolve to be a
tireless leader, resumed recording his own sermons

started a serious adult choir practice and
handpicked couples to start a youth group

CHAPTER 62 – New Year's Eve Wedding

Tony and Susan have been given permission to marry

Esther and I would be allowed to go to the wedding, but
first, shopping at the new Metro Center Mall in Phoenix

looking for dresses, they would be pink, most of
our clothes were hand sewn, rarely something new

miles of saguaro cactus lined the winding highway
threading the starkness of the hills and ravines

driving toward a small desert mountain called Gavilan
distinct, monumental, sitting right near Interstate 17

when the sun laid just right, illuminated some places
and made shadows in others, I could see his sharp

craggy features, Ramses II, imperial nose pointed at the
heavens, neatly stuffed with black peppercorns, a priestly

mummification hack to prevent nasal collapse, this was
my secret imagined story, an Egyptian Pharaoh staring at

the sky in an Arizona desert, whimsical magic, to see a thing
no one else could see, murmured hello, smiled secretly

as we flew by, on the way to buy pink chiffon dresses

The wedding was exciting and beautiful

a rare treat for Esther and I, dressed in
expensive new dresses, pink and frothy
hair done adult style in a poofed coiffure

both bride and groom, blue eyed, with
naturally curly blonde hair, amazingly alike
a quiet ceremony in Sister Nita's trailer

there would be a large reception, doubled for
a New Year Celebration, would not start until late
held at The Dining Hall, we were not allowed to go

it wasn't until later we understood why, they were
drinking pink champagne, we'd all heard the words of
the Prophet, thunderous sermons on the evils of drink

"You will notice when people begin to get together, first thing you know, it begins to bring in devices for recreation, from gambling, into drinking, drinking into prostitution, breaking of homes, marriage, divorce, then murder, it just keeps growing, growing, growing like a chain with no end."

walking past The Dining Hall, saw one of the
adults fall out of the back window into
the grass, and others hooting from the trees

intensified brewing inner conflict, injustice
buzzed over my scalp, like a swarm of angry bees
kids were humiliated, punished, and ostracized

for childish infractions, or incarcerated
in the blackness of the root cellars for enjoying
innocent fun, expected to know and quote

the Prophet on points of evil and the things
we are forbidden to do while adults cavorted and
willingly disobeyed the words of the Prophet

it was futile rage, burning incandescently
"Growing, growing, growing, like a chain with no end!"

CHAPTER 63 – Stolen Books

I turned 13 in 1974 and started 8th grade

new library rule, three books only
to feed the ravenous hunger in

my emerging brain, my seeking heart
and the dark simmering place in my belly

supply chain failing me, full library
hundreds, thousands, of books

check out only three, to satisfy
me for two weeks, what would I do?

I could not take them home any longer
they had to be read at school

my only interest, escape my awful
life, delve into transient possibility

books were just sitting there
looking for me, I would *take* them

not watched carefully
at school, checked out three

carried out many more, under
fold of coat or sweater

I built a library of my own
school locker crammed full

every inch bulging with books
no room for pencils, pens or

assignments, I stuffed those

in brown bags, stored them on

an empty shelf in the back
closet of my homeroom

inevitable disaster, narrow
school locker, unable to contain

another item, betrayed me
spat books, crashing, cascading

splayed across the hall, a colorful
cobbled path of books, straight to the

classroom door of Mrs. Dardis, tiny
old lady, immediate fury directed at me

standing, ruddy faced, in a pile of books
silently, stupidly embarrassed

scolded in front of other students
released from class, crowding the halls

she'd been looking for one of the books
from her personal classroom collection

another teacher with no insight
sent me walking home with a letter

now I'm a thief as well as a liar
I have *"stolen"* more than 70 books

secreted them in my locker
parents required to respond

sneaked around the back through
the rocks to mama, as usual

dozing heavily on the couch, this

time I can't let her rest peacefully

shook her gently, again and again
then roughly, clutched her shoulder

"Mama! Wake up…….you have to wake up!"

fear, like a butter churn, chuffing in
my midsection, hampered my patience

"Please mama, wake up! You have to help me!"

mama woke, groggy, sat up, blinked
rubbed her hands over her face

stumbled to the bathroom
came back, face freshly washed

read the letter, stood thinking
paced a bit, came to decision

"Meet me across the creek by Purcell's. We'll go back to the school right now."

kind fates, no interference
mama met me, steady, determined

briskly, we walked back to the
school and mama saved my ass

shook that letter at the principle
wanted to know how *borrowed* books

never left school property, and
now safely returned to the library

could be stolen? Stupendous
moments, mama reigned

took spindly grey man to task

questioned his job, if not

to put books in the hands
of eager readers, case dismissed

slowly, taking precious time
we walked back to the entrance

of The Park, stood beneath
the large red ochre sign

mama quietly, sadly, touched
the scattered freckles on my nose

like she did when I was her baby
spoke softly, *"Debbie Dee"*

I moved away, walking backwards
looking at her through a wash

of shimmering tears, heart full of
bitter affection, dreadful impotence

both of us returned to purgatory

She kept them in a basket by the couch

Good Housekeeping
magazines, I might never
have ventured a look
but like a starving
dog, I was digging for
sustenance in any
available midden heap
of course, reading
my sister's magazines
was strictly forbidden
and resentment
stewed in my gut
simmering pottage

she could read
"Worldly trash"
look at brightly
made up housewives
browse stupid ads
for products, drink
wine, swallow pills
while I was restricted
to the Bible and
recorded sermons
grinding work
endless rebuke
constant failure

but nestled in
those glossy pages
similar to *"Mara Daughter of The Nile"*
adventure and romance
a campy gem, *"Moonraker's Bride"*
set during the boxer
rebellion in China
considered adult
romantic fiction, but I

left age-related books
behind a long time ago
immediately
captivated, I sank
into familiar, beloved
cadence, identified
with characters
settings, rising action
mysterious riddles
conflict, catastrophe
and............

No way!

only half of the
story in this edition
the rest would follow
next month
a real conundrum
shook myself from
mists of fiction
carefully replaced
the magazine
exactly as I found it
and immediately
began to count
the days until
the next one arrived

she never knew I
slaked my thirst with her
monthly subscription
for many, many months
guzzled under cover
of night in the
dimly lit bubble
beneath my blankets

sneakily replaced
before dawn, no
evidence of my sin visible

Blessed with sweet dimples, bubbly giggle, long curls, and

intuitive blue eyes, full
of innocent mischief
my little niece, now more
like my little sister

unable to commiserate
but still, endearing
ordered to teach her
a selected scripture

for Sunday morning
pre-school class in
The Chapel, the younger
children would gather

to recite several scriptures
for *The Servant of The Lord*
frustrating new task
failure was not an option

a live-in nanny of sorts
I saw to her bath, rubbed
her down with baby lotion
carefully rolled her long

hair with foam curlers
tucked her into bed,
solicited her silence
when I read forbidden

books under the covers
bath time, a perfect
opportunity to
memorize scriptures

little brother asleep
parents gone for the

evening, four lines of
verse, lots of stumbling

pauses, starts and stops
complete frustration in
just a few minutes
they were simple words

angrily frustrated, unable to
recognize this as impatience
I yanked on her long curls
produced immediate tears

worse was done to me
so I pushed for renewed
effort, finally one
line remembered

out of the tub, dressed
for bed, continued on to
working the second line
while rolling her hair

frustrated, afraid of failure
I rolled up a towel and
snapped her leg
left a livid red welt

Johnny and Tony used to
tease and snap towels at us
sordid shame mixed
with a sense of relief

and accomplishment
when she finally recited
the verse almost perfectly
excellent result, she became

a shining example in

The Chapel Sunday school
Brother Leo watching
puffy, pasty, oversized

eyes drooping, voiced
garbled, words slurred
could hardly pretend
to be interested

she recited her verse
without a stumble, as
expected but I realized
I crossed a line, dipped

my cup in the oily brew
of coerced obedience
became like one of
the adults I abhorred

for blindly following
instruction, using threat
and fear to produce
expected results, deep

inside, I checked a box
never again, much too
great, the price for
my failure and inability to

align with the expected
outcome, I saved myself
at the expense of another
softer, less defiled soul

CHAPTER 64 – Bible Trivia

As a teen I was allowed to go to youth group, we

gathered in different homes
for reading the Bible
and listening to
Brother Leo's taped
sermons, annoying
disturbing, his voice
thick and slurred
often made no sense

we drank soda
ate chips and dips
girls brought cookies
or rice crispy treats
the couple in charge
Brother Eddie and Sister Alice
they were kind and enjoyed
creating fun ways
to learn and enjoy
what they believed
to be critical information
directly linked to salvation

I loved the group
I was rarely in
trouble anymore
Brother Leo wasn't
healthy enough to continue
his tyranny on a regular
basis, so the adults
fell into a lull as well
and life in The Park
became more friendly
and constructive
it was decided

youth group would do a
Bible Trivia Challenge

the winner would
receive a brand new
Thompson Chain
Reference Bible, the
King James Version from
BB Kirkbride Bible Company
it was passed around
in its beautiful
box for all to see
expensive supple brown
leather binding
each book of the Bible
tabbed with a
golden thumb inset
to be easily referenced

given a set of scriptures
to read in preparation for
the next youth meeting
much of it already deeply
ingrained, I studied and read
the assignment anyway
with great intent
and eager anticipation

the questions started
they seemed too easy
eventually they
got harder, but none
I couldn't answer
full of delighted
excitement
bouncing in my chair
eventually, I was
required to wait
until no one else could

answer the question
an enlightening experience
taught me a great deal
changed my life

I learned a thing about
myself, give me something
to read and study, I will
never forget it, I could close
my eyes and see it on the page
if I wrote it once, even better
still, vaguely surprised
kids who had been raised
the same way I was
could not answer
questions about things
we'd heard all our lives
for me it was
like breathing in
and breathing out

I won that beautiful Bible
in just two meetings
full of satisfied happiness
I couldn't take to heart, a
flabbergasted Brother Eddie
who so far, only knew
me as a problem child
the one labeled *"Serpent's seed"*

I felt something
I'd never felt before
recognition for
a job well done
I liked it, wanted more
set my sights
on getting more
praise and validation
decided I would

do everything
every chore
every assignment
every job perfectly

no room for any
poor outcomes
or failure

CHAPTER 65 – Nathan and Dipsey Doodle

Like most teen girls, even in The Park

everyone had a silly crush on somebody
such excitement and drama, we talked while
mopping floors and making sandwiches
packing lunches for the Junior High kids

unable to identify with boys in The Park
the other girls thought I was weird
but I had a secret crush of my own
I knew him from school, a local boy

from a large family of ranchers
lived out around Spider Ranch, they
had a big orchard where we went to
pick apples every now and then

he lost his leg when he was barely
two years old, some kind of gun
accident but nothing stood in his
way, in spite of his loss, I could not

see it as a handicap, he was beautiful
exotic, dark skinned, rumpled black hair
brown eyes, western clothes and
belt buckle, metal crutch buried in his

armpit, an extension of his body
almost alive in its own right, there
was nothing he couldn't do, ride
rope, high jump, roller skate

he was absolutely remarkable
I was deeply enamored, he of course

knew me only as one of the
weird kids from the commune

of "*Jesus Freaks*"

There was another set of twins at Prescott Junior High

boys, Shelly and Kelly, also
from a local ranch family

7th and 8th grade guitar
class together, sitting

in the very last row
Esther and I had a wicked

running, name calling
event with them

always old country
blue jeans, western shirts

cowboy boots, and big
shiny shiny belt buckles

We called them
"Beer Belly Kelly and Pot Belly Shelly"

I don't think our name
calling stuck to them

but their name calling
surely stuck to us

mostly, they called us
"The Dipsey Doodle Daultons"

I asked them once, what
that meant, turns out

it was some kind of
sweet pineapple cake

a lifetime later, Esther's
last words *"I love you Doodle"*

CHAPTER 66 – Mr. Neely

Early 1974, 8th grade, my homeroom teacher

a real gentleman
with salt and pepper hair
he wore glasses above
short neat beard
caught me reading a book
in Social Studies class
tucked inside my
large text book

"Dune" I was deeply
entranced with the
"Bene Gesserit, Maud 'dib"
and *"Kwisatz Haderach"*
I could not take *any* book
home with me, but
this one would have
been considered
deeply heretical

moments passed
before I realized he
was talking to me
when he tapped me
on the shoulder
with a ruler, I startled
dropped my text book
and the secret book

face reddened
acutely embarrassed
listening to the
other kids snickering
"Am I boring you, young lady"
stammered, shrugged

reluctantly handed
over my book

he held it until after class
met me up front
"Why do you read in class? You have hours to read at home after school."
still embarrassed
afraid of the trouble
I'd be in, I explained
begged him not to
cause trouble for me

he did the opposite
asked me how many
many books I needed
"Five, at least five"
sent me home with
a note, I must read five
books every week, submit
a book report to him
for each of them

I discovered, this
intuitive, kind teacher
kept beanie hats available
in his class room for
the boys of The Park
to cover the shame of
their shaved heads
a common punishment
for them, definitely
not considered
cool in the 60s and 70s

for me, his simple solution
worked amazingly well
my sister looked hard at the note
and that was that
I was *free…. free…. free*

to read whatever
I wanted, she never
looked at another book
I brought home

this seemed to be
happening in most
homes, adults
more pressingly
concerned with
failing leadership
less concerned with
disobedient kids
gradually, we enjoyed
a tiny reprieve
from absolute control

CHAPTER 67 – Whiskey Sour

In the back corner of the store room

in The Dining Hall
sent to get canned beans
I overheard a conversation
between two of the Brothers
standing in the dimly lit
hall near the phone, one
of them talked about
having dinner with
Brother Leo and
some other Brothers
in a local restaurant
El Chapparal

my heart started to
beat a little faster
what should I do?
resolved to be very quiet
stay put until I could
get clear to return
back down to the stoves

they talked in quiet
tones, insistent
and frustrated
"I'm telling you he was drunk…. I was embarrassed."
my ears perked up
I concentrated hard
really wanted to hear
their conversation
some of them
had tried to dissuade
further intoxication
"He sent me to the bar to order another Whiskey Sour in the name of The Lord Jesus Christ."

well, I knew what
whiskey was but had
no reference for
"A whiskey sour"
second man asked
"Did ya do it?"
strained hard to hear
lowered voices
"Well, no, of course not! I got him another drink but I didn't say that."
weird feeling in
my stomach, what
are we doing here?

what did this mean
for all of us?
what is the meaning
of our existence
in this regimented
place, separate from
the world and its vices?
quiet words again
"This is wrong and we need to do something about it."
second Brother agreed
"We'll talk about it. You're right. It needs to stop."

I waited until
they walked back
to the lower area
and made their way
into the dinner line
before coming
out of my corner
and rushing to
deliver the beans
wryly aware of
the benefits
of being a non-entity
unimportant
invisible

CHAPTER 68 – Strange Covenants

As working teens, we could feel unrest, and we overheard growing concern

adults in The Park becoming
ever more restless
disquieted
with events obviously
contradictory to the
teachings of the Prophet
antithetical to their
personal convictions
like many people
with lives invested
in a preordained outcome
which has not occurred

having hung their hopes
their faith, and
eternal destination
on a life in The Park
they clung to anything that
might help them keep
disappointment
desperation, *failure*
at bay, but misgivings grew
uncertainty, doubt in our cause

everyone, including the kids
recognized deterioration
in *The Servant of The Lord*
conversely, we were
thankful for it
but he continued
to manipulate and control
using fear, even as his
addictions grew
and he became ever

more self-indulgent

appearing for meals
impaired, demanding to be
chauffeured into town
by followers, to imbibe
at various establishments
his sexual proclivities
began to worm
into his doctrine
he insisted upon his
first covenant
the *"White Ribbon Covenant"*

men were required to
abstain from sexual relations
with their wives for
several months
placing the white ribbon
in the pages of their Bible
to mark acceptance
dedication to this covenant
followed closely
by the very peculiar
"Eliezer Covenant"

Abraham said unto his servant, Eliezer, who had charge over his house

"Put your hand under my thigh, and I will make you swear by the Lord, the God of heaven and earth……"

Biblical premise for
the taking of oaths
on the loins of the master
timeless and believable
in the world of men
swearing on blessed seed

nothing so sacred as testes
evident masculinity
but *The Servant of the Lord*
chose to extrapolate
this meant the
organ of circumcision

that scepter used
like banal meaty
providence to rule over
the world and women
must be held as
sacred object to be
sworn upon

influence and power
wielded for so long
gave him ability to
manipulate men
desiring righteousness
above all else
first, teaching
sexuality
decreases morality
slyly hold them there
with spiritual covenant
then bring them to

a special meeting
extract a vow
upon the loins of
the master, a resultant
spiritual ejaculation
men with adult brains
and the power to say no
allowed themselves
to become victims
of the puppeteer
much as the children
had been for many years

he jerked their strings
watched the resultant gambol
men seeking a greater
connection to God
instead indulged the
sexual needs of a man
perpetually warped
his desires frustrated
by his choices

he wanted power
and influence, control
as a religious leader
in a fundamental
sect with room only
to disavow
such inclinations

he belonged in the halls
of infamy, inhabited
for eons by religious men
who took the cloth
and used children
available among faithful
parishioners
who sat in confession

while their children
were robbed of things
parents are meant to ensure

innocence, and a childhood
free of monsters
Brother Leo Mercier
was not satisfied
with abusing the children
he needed a deed
to eclipse any
inclination to query
halt any reaction to
sacred boundaries crossed

his deplorable plan backfired
men realized what
they had been led into
one of the young men
newly married
held abstinent for months
subjected to this tactic
bashed his head through a
glass medicine cabinet

my family, my brothers
began to talk
returned to their first absolute
The Message
found what they needed
to make the break, of course
a quote from William Branham

"Have you ever noticed that people who lead others astray, bind them closely to themselves by fear? They say if the people don't do what they say or if they leave, then destruction will follow. Don't put your confidence in that man, you leave that man."

My brother's wife, slapped her
hand down on the table

exclaimed, *"That's nothing but the truth!"*
and just like that
life as I knew it imploded
The Park split right in half
those still following Brother Leo
and those who were done with him

CHAPTER 69 – Division and Chaos

Adults of The Park became embroiled in debate

Brother Leo cowered, stayed out of sight
served by a few who remained faithful
while the majority raged at each other

gathering in different family homes
to talk doctrine, faith, and next steps
half the group believed we should stay

faithful to Brother Leo, to our great achievement
separation from the world, the other half
argued, Brother Leo betrayed us all and we

needed to return to teachings of the Prophet
the pressing question, *"Who will lead us?"*
I heard Brother Will, our frequent chastiser

"Not that dirty rotten drinkin, druggin, bastard!"

as vehement and dedicated now, to his
downfall as he had been to supporting him
two factions of adults so embittered, betrayed

they never recognized how this might affect
their children, we had never seen division like this
Brother Leo ruled like God, still we had no voice

adults ceased to care what the kids were doing
overnight, all the rules disappeared, from
where I lived, who I lived with, how I rolled my hair

where my hemline should be, what kind of
shoes I wore, when I ate, what I ate, the way
I walked, or sat, what I read, how I talked,

invasion of intimate privacies, all psychotic
control over my life, my breath, my being
completely gone, order and regimentation

gone, no meals prepared at The Dining Hall
or The Toddle House, the kids figured out
quickly there was no one at the helm

of this rapidly sinking ship and the whole
bunch of us took immediate advantage
only a few months left of the school year

but we stopped going, boys were out
riding bikes until all hours, girls skated on
the Big Patio until dark, we raided lunch stores

in both food halls, hostess cupcakes and snoballs,
cracker jacks, potato chips, and candy bars
holed up in rocky forts, indulging a new sense

of autonomy to do what we wanted, buried
the niggling insecurity of chaos and uncertainty
in the joy of independent actions and desires

we reveled in the chain lightning change
grabbed onto the tail of meteoric freedom
governed ourselves, awaiting the outcome

of this split and the final days of The Park

CHAPTER 70 - Going Home Again

I decided I was going back home

daddy and mama
happened to be gone
visiting relatives
in Kentucky when the
big split happened
too much time
had passed to go back
to Herb and Grace

I would be home
when they got back
told my sister on
the way out the door
she just nodded

returned to the old
blue and white trailer
almost five years older
bearing more scars
everything I owned
still fit in a garbage bag

Sharon was already
there, I hung
my clothes in the
closet, undies and socks
back in my old drawer
the two of us waited
for Esther to show up
but she didn't

should've known
it wouldn't be easy
she was stuck

with a family still
supporting Brother Leo
they wouldn't let her leave

my family united
in a way I had
not experienced
since I was very young
back when we
were still Daulton's
when daddy strummed
his guitar and sang
in the evenings
when the kids and
grandkids gathered
to enjoy country kin
and home cooking

my older brothers
decided *"We're goin to get Esther"*
we walked there together
right next door to
Brother Leo's trailer
I couldn't keep
from looking over
at his bathroom window
wondered
if he was watching

the Brother
of the house met
us as we arrived
he stepped out
and closed the door
behind him
"This is where The Servant of the Lord placed her, this is where she will stay."

my brothers closed
on him, one of them

reached behind him
opened the door
"Girls, get on in there and get your sister."
and stood holding
the door open

possibly the Brother
didn't reckon any
of them would actually
go against Brother Leo
but his choices diminished
with three of our older
brothers involved

we scuttled around
the men, to find her
sitting on the bed
in the room she
shared with their daughter
nervous, biting her
fingernails bloody

we left without any
of her things, other than
what she was wearing
didn't matter, we
didn't care, we were
free, finally free
we got them later
when even the few
still faithful to
Brother Leo
abandoned him

daddy and mama
got home and
our life started over
they were nearing
sixty years old

with three teenage
daughters at home

fighting over showers
bathroom time
clothes, and the
ever-loving radio, now
some music was allowed
we still trekked to
the washhouse to do
laundry, like we did when
we were little, I was just
leaving when one of the
Sisters came in with
her laundry, she
stopped me at the door

put her basket down
and took my hands
looked into my eyes
and sincerely apologized
for everything that
happened to me when
I was living in her house

asked me to forgive
her part in what she
described as the
injustice of things
that haunted her
told me she paid, her
maternal heart broken by
her own child's suffering

she was the single
adult of The Park
thought to ask
forgiveness from a child
that day is like a

crystal songbird, held
in a translucent cage

I keep it tucked
away for re-examining
it was the first day
of my life, I was assigned
real value and
my forgiveness was
worth asking for

CHAPTER 71 – Leaving Pine Lawn Trailer Ranch

Over the next several months, folks began pulling trailers out of The Park

ripping up beautiful
flagstone patios
and sidewalks
stone walls and flower
beds, pushed over
shoved aside
gaping holes left
in our little commune

no sign of Brother Leo
he hid in his home
while dissolution
happened around him
he was completely
abandoned, not
one soul stuck by
him in the end

we never went
back to school, daddy
sold machinery
vehicles, and tools
banked everything
for our future, finally
he sold the old
blue and white striped
Kentuckian, bought a
small travel trailer

planned to move us
to Flagstaff
my oldest brother
had some property
up there, and a
double wide trailer

already set up
I walked the familiar
trails, hiked the winding
trail up into the
granite boulders, sat in
a split between two
huge monoliths

looked down over
The Park, silently
gazed over each trailer space
preserved the names of every
man, woman, and child who lived
there, wondered at the
complete disconnect
how each family chose
to go different ways

I had no memories
before The Park
Esther and I just turned
fourteen years old
we'd known these people
for every minute
of our lives, and now
all was changing, I
knew I'd never forget
recognized…someday
I would have a thing
or two to say about all of this

I lifted my face to the sun
enjoyed the breeze
as it lifted my long hair
off my shoulders
I felt the whip and snap
of it flying behind me
like a battle flag
I burst from my chrysalis

and winged outward
toward that big question mark

a world outside The Park

EPILOGUE

Almost seven years later, January of 1982

I returned to Prescott
finally going to college
a trailblazing victory
gained one skirmish
at a time, waged with
manipulations and
actions I knew my parents
could not abide
desperate to produce
specific results, I began dating
a married man

this elicited exactly what
I hoped for, my Godly
conservative parents
preferred college to
adultery, fornication
and irredeemable sin
totally understood by now
there are things that
cannot be forgiven, even
by the one who forgives all

everything I gambled
fell clinking into place
my concerned family
coughed up 672 dollars
and sent me to live with
my brother in Chino Valley
somewhat near the school
I showed up for
class, seven days late
denied at registration
the semester already started
no high school, no SAT's

no idea one cannot
register to go to college
just because they want to

stubbornly, I refused to leave
asked to talk to the guy
in charge of the college
following a persistent
slightly defiant parlay with
the man I *now* knew as the Dean
we reached an accord
thankful for yet another
intuitive educator

I would start the semester
late, take the college
classes he assigned
and make the Dean's list
those tasks completed, I
could sit for my GED and
SATs in the summer, start
the Nursing Program in the fall

he walked me to
my first class, English 101
followed by Algebra, Biology
Chemistry, and Sociology
released me to sink or swim
like an athlete on the starting block
I plunged in, given the
directive, only the goal in sight

I loved English, wrote
my term paper with excruciatingly
profound commiseration, kinship
with an ordinary woman, a sinner
caught in extraordinary
circumstances, *Hester Prynne*
condemned by her puritanical

neighbors, unbroken by her trials

Hawthorne's *"The Scarlet Letter"*

Late May 1982, I had the newspaper in my hands

proof, my name published
alongside other students
also made the Dean's list

not sure the Dean expected this
outcome, but he kept his word
cautioned me I would need

to do all of my pre-requisites
along with the 2-year program
to make for some 14 to 17

credit hours per semester, and
I'd need to do summer classes
as well *"No worries, I can do it!"*

he put my name on the roster
for the September program, I was
heartily stoked to go and buy the

required ugly white dress and shoes
my uniform was complete with a
long wacky apron, had a hole right

in the middle for my head, fastened
on all the way down the front and
the back, a dimpled bulge at every

buttonhole, trimmed in hunter green
a beaming lumpy caterpillar, I was
dressed in the school colors for the

Yavapai College Nursing Program

Clinical rotations started for Nursing students at

Yavapai Regional Medical Center
where the five of us
had tonsillectomies
all those years ago
third floor nursing station
eager for patients of my own

a sour faced old nurse
tired of students
messing with her mojo
taking her metered time
brusquely, she handed me
a sheet of paper, pointed
to the patient chart rack
"Go read your patient charts, take notes."

four names, black and bug like
crawling across my list
name…
name…
name…
Mercier, Leo W….

what volcanic irony
this name on
my clinical assignment
never even thought
to recuse myself
from his bedside

breathing too fast
lips numb, tingling
not seething hatred, but *fear*
my knees locked in
robotic forward direction
I ambulated the antiseptically
gleaming hall, to the door

of a four-bed ward
my patients, each
with different afflictions

Behind curtain #2, Brother Leo W. Mercier

AKA: *The Servant of The Lord*

mortal, born of a woman
pushed mewling
from the pathos
of her womb
the ancient Spinners
gouged his soft fontanelle
opened his unformed skull
like a bloody tulip
needled in narcissism
sadism, and perversion
enhanced
what was already
sown there, some
deep ancestral evil
now they stand ready
to snip his life thread

his Pentecostal mama
tranced her infant
with painted eyes
stuttered red lipped
glossolalia into
ears already pricked
to malevolent darkness
crooned dominion
in her lullabies
laid beneath his feet
a promenade
bloody bone shards
to walk upon
shattered children
like Jesus
walked upon water

Brother Leo Mercier

the winding serpent
of my childhood
obscene lurker in
my shadowed brain
skin walker from
my nightmares
abandoned
by his followers
friends and family
an empty ghost vessel
stranded in the hospital bed
where he ran himself aground

He rested with his head slightly elevated

heavy lidded, jaundiced, once portly
brown skin folds now flapping sails
a wrinkled carcass, aware I could
skin, gut, and hang him to bleed out
with less pity than I felt for
any beast we filled our bellies with

no perfumed cloud permeates
his decay, his breath not cinnamon
but essence of rancid mealworms
efficiently, I turned him side to side
cleansed away the familiar scent
of bloody slaughter, tucked him in
with fresh linens and pillows
used him, rotting meat, to learn
my craft, reveled in my ability
and solid oxen strength

he, a dying mammal received
my trepidatious, attuned observation
ripples fanned across my consciousness
unanticipated, *forgiveness* sparked in
cold charred coals, and like the *Holy Ghost*
rose, a scintillating specter from the
deeply felt pain of old betrayals

slyly, eyes half mast, he said
"I know who you are."
delusional despot assumed I was still a
fragile child, to be bound by his words
spoke as if he mattered to me, said all of us
would return to him, unable to live in
this world without his guidance
I listened, looked down on him, and answered

*"I know who you are…and I forgive you.
I will take good care of you*

and then I will walk away from you."

my carapaced heart
understood, I would lose
nothing and gain forever
that ridged old eschar
of fear ripped away
leaving fresh and pink
the tender entity underneath
to granulate new power

knees stable now, sent to
the lab by my preceptor to
collect cold blood in squashy bags
diligently processed, compared
type tags with the blood bank
then again with preceptor
doubly sure the type
wouldn't kill him, knew
he would die anyway
hooded reaper already
in his shadow
carefully we dripped warm
timed ruby life into his ruin
transfused his living corpse

I felt no tender brow stroking concern
gave him what he created in me
decreased empathy, concrete efficiency
consuming fear of *The Servant of The Lord,* gone

in my youthful vitality, the ignorance
of my bliss, I believed
there was nothing left to glint
in the setting suns on my horizons
no monster to stomp the
landmines in my dreamscape

Folks may ask why I waited so long to tell my story. I love my family and have no desire to hurt them or undermine their faith with researchable facts. I navigated my own path and remained silent. I didn't ask burning questions, never disturbed their stony absolute with undeniable evidence. I was free to listen to or read misguided sermons, but as a woman deemed unworthy to question or investigate. The Message conjectures, every word Branham spoke from the pulpit, under the anointing, came directly from God. *"These pretty faced women is lower in the sight of God, ten million times, than an old slut dog or a sow. Every sin was ever on earth was caused by a woman. That's it exactly!"* His disciple bruised my soul with these words. His intent, to sow an arable field with insecurity and decreased self-worth.

My words are not the voice of God but they will be here for people to read long after I am gone. Infinity, reaped from the grist of my life. I have never experienced anything so heart grinding, so devastating, so completely intolerable, as watching my twin sister die, afraid of a transition we all make, unable to speak of death, even with me, her embryonic soulmate. When her heartbeat slowed and stumbled and I felt her impending demise, cutting through that fog, like a chariot race in my skull, Alexis de Tocqueville's timeless words. *"The evil that one endures patiently because it seems inevitable, becomes unbearable the moment its elimination becomes conceivable."*

I had to speak out, shake the tree, rattle this androcentric religion, for surely these good people who elevate a man, blood and bone, to the *"Voice of God"* find him incapable of vanity, false pride, and the ability to perpetuate a lie, have fallen for the oldest human scam. They have abandoned their divine right to touch the heart of God without a skin wrapped intermediary, mortal and fallible as they are. I seek God on my own, like I did when I was a child and cried for his protection, when I begged him to spare my mind even as my body was abused, my soul robbed of innocence, and sweet childlike faith was ripped from my heart.

When I face the transition of death, I will emulate mama, surrounded by her children and grandchildren, white haired, venerated, unafraid, and radiant. Serenely ready for the beautiful transition she earned with silent work, wisdom, and her maternal heart. I will not rail and struggle against the end of a life well lived. I will not whisper the desolate words I heard from my daddy in his final days, "Brother Branham lied to me. I have been betrayed."

ACKNOWLEDGEMENTS

My heartfelt thanks and acknowledgement to Write by Night, David and Justine Duhr, who took my huge mess of an unfinished manuscript and paired me up with the wonderful and talented, John Sibley Williams, the award-winning poet. He helped me streamline and perfect my clumsy life project. Much love and thanks to my husband, Ron Thibodeau, who suffered through many of these losses with me, experienced this exposure therapy with me, endured all of my fears, my good memories, anguished memories, my rants, my tears, old pain, new pain, and finally solid resolution. To Christian Chiba, my first wild heartfelt, revolutionary love, we defied convention and the dictates of my religious upbringing. To my son Ronin Chiba, the blue-eyed boy who made me a mama, tilted my planet, and who has always listened without judgement. To Fumiko Chiba Tipping, my baby girl, my therapist, she kept me level and offered words of advice beyond her years. Both love me still, in spite of my many parental mistakes. To my techy second son, Roger Tipping, who helped me figure out how to format and manage my manuscript. To Dr. Joe Dispenza who gave me, *"Breaking the Habit of being Yourself,"* essential quantum science I needed to overcome doubt, write my story, and create my future reality.

Figure 1 Daddy, Mama, JimEd, Marietta, Alberta, Doris, Joseph, & Jerry, the Older siblings

Figure 2 Daulton Family Kentucky October 1961

Figure 3 Daddy and Mama WWI

Figure 5 Esther & Deborah

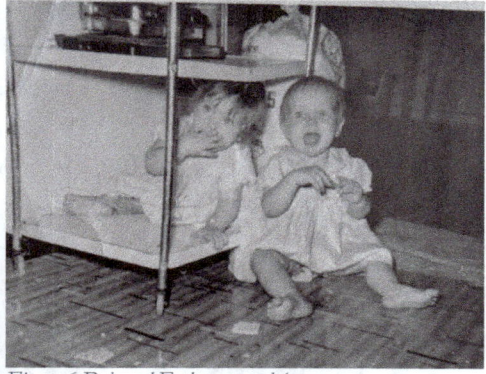

Figure 6 Deb and Esther around 1 year

Figure 4 Esther, Deborah, Mark Edward & The Kentuckian

Figure 7 Sister Hattie and Mama

Figure 9 Daddy and Mama, motorcycle parked on the patio

Figure 8 Leo Mercier, William Branham, Gene Goad

Figure 10 Early Blissful Days in The Dining Hall-Leo Mercier standing hand on Gene Goad's shoulder

Figure 11 Leo Mercier & William Branham

Figure 12 William Branham & Leo Mercier

Figure 14 William Branham and Leo Mercier

Figure 13 William Branham and Leo Mercier

Figure 17 William Branham & Gene Goad

Figure 18 Leo, Gene, & Tony

Figure 16 Leo & Johnny

Figure 15 Leo, Gene, & Danny Bill

Figure 21 Esther, Miriam, Eliabeth, Anna, Deborah, and Salome

Figure 20 Deb & Hannah Hair still Growing 1972

Figure 19 Park Kids at Gran Canyon Caverns

Figure 22 Herb & Grace Russian Party

Figure 23 Back row, 12 yrs old age of accountabily-adult hair style-Angela, Becky, Esther, and Deborah

Figure 24 Herb and Grace

Figure 25 Herb and Grace

Figure 26 The way the creek looked in the 60's

Figure 27 Big Patio Converted to a Garage and the Hangin Tree

Figure 28 Daulton Patio -built 1963

Figure 29 One of the old sidewalks behind our trailer.

Figure 30 What is left of the Root Cellars in 2021

ABOUT THE AUTHOR

Though her early years were profoundly traumatic, Deborah Daulton Thibodeau's biography may sound unremarkable: Born into a large, God-fearing Southern family; worked in emergency nursing for more than thirty years; married twice, with kids, grandkids, and pets.

What's missing from this version of Deborah's bio is the very ground she covers in her memoir-in-verse, *The Serpent's Tail*: Her childhood spent in a religious cult. She details the years of mental, physical, and often sexualized abuse she suffered at the hands of Brother Leo Mercier and his followers, all bound by devoted adherence to *"The Message"* and the *"Prophet of the Hour,"* Reverend William Marrion Branham.

Like many post-war families, Ed and Bessie Daulton of Pulaski County, Kentucky, found purpose in Pentecostal revival. They moved out West to live in righteous seclusion and await the second coming of Christ, their twelve children in tow, including one-year-old Deborah and her twin sister, Esther. The Daultons landed in Prescott, Arizona, and lived happily for a few years. Soon Ed and Bessie's individual will and independent thoughts were subverted by Brother Leo Mercier, self-proclaimed *"Servant of the Lord and Shepherd"* of The Park. Soon he wrested control over teaching and disciplining the children, and before long, the five youngest Daulton children were handed off to be raised by other cult members.

When The Park split, the children had endured thirteen years of indoctrination and brutality, but they weren't out of the woods. The Daultons moved to Flagstaff but continued to attend a church within the religion, with continued fundamentalist expectations for women.

Deborah, eager for an escape from this prescribed life, learned to compartmentalize post-traumatic night terrors and adjustment disorders, educated herself in secret, procuring books and hiding them, taking night classes. Before turning eighteen, Deborah stunned the family by taking a job as an ER Tech. She stunned them again by enrolling in college, and then, the ultimate betrayal, she dated and married a man outside the church.

Esther never recovered from the trauma of their childhood. The last years of her life were full of conflict, and she self-medicated with alcohol. Cancer claimed her in 2013, but her childhood in The Park was the more accurate cause of death.

Reeling from her twin's death, Deborah made the life-altering decision to write *The Serpent's Tail*. She desired, above all else, to give children of The Park, many who have suffered similar post-traumatic disorders and subsequent life events, the voice they never had, to pave the way for them to speak after 48 years of silence. Deborah left the ER to work with Veterans suffering from PTSD, moral injury, mental illness, alcoholism, and drug-induced psychosis.

    Today Deborah still lives and works in the Prescott Quad Cities area with her husband Ron, several of their adult children, and seven grandchildren, a great treasure she never believed she'd have as a child. They share their home with Puma, a very spoiled and rotund black cat. When they are not enjoying the local community and events or hiking the local trails, she and Ron look for new kayaking adventures.

www.ingramcontent.com/pod-product-compliance
Lightning Source LLC
Chambersburg PA
CBHW071226070526
44583CB00017B/2062